I0816351

WHAT FOR

Mauricio Macri

WHAT FOR

Work edited in collaboration with Editorial Planeta – Argentina

Original title: *Para qué*

Translated by: María Paula Miguel y Martínez
Cover adaptation: Genoveva Saavedra García

Publishing house PLANETA M.R.
Avenida Presidente Masarik núm. 111,
Piso 2, Polanco V Sección, Miguel Hidalgo
C.P. 11560, Ciudad de México
www.planetadelibros.com.mx

First edition: October 2023
ISBN: 978-607-39-0432-2

Printed in Litográfica Ingramex, S.A. de C.V.
Centeno núm. 162-1, colonia Granjas Esmeralda, Ciudad de México
Printed and made in Mexico - *Impreso y hecho en México*

To Alfredo, my grandson, who will live
in a better Argentina.

Contents

PART ONE
Leadership
From Sideco to Boca

PART TWO
Power

The City and the Nation

If—

If you can keep your head when all about you
Are losing theirs and blaming it on you;
If you can trust yourself when all men doubt you,
But make allowance for their doubting too;
If you can wait and not be tired by waiting,
Or being lied about, don't deal in lies,
Or being hated don't give way to hating,
And yet don't look too good, nor talk too wise;

If you can dream—and not make dreams your master;
If you can think—and not make thoughts your aim;
If you can meet with Triumph and Disaster
And treat those two impostors just the same;
If you can bear to hear the truth you've spoken
Twisted by knaves to make a trap for fools,
Or watch the things you gave your life to, broken,
And stoop and build 'em up with worn-out tools;

If you can make one heap of all your winnings
And risk it on one turn of pitch-and-toss,
And lose, and start again at your beginnings
And never breathe a word about your loss;
If you can force your heart and nerve and sinew

To serve your turn long after they are gone,
And so hold on when there is nothing in you
Except the Will which says to them: "Hold on!"

If you can talk with crowds and keep your virtue,
Or walk with Kings—nor lose the common touch;
If neither foes nor loving friends can hurt you;
If all men count with you, but none too much;
If you can fill the unforgiving minute
With sixty seconds' worth of distance run,
Yours is the Earth and everything that's in it,
And—which is more—you'll be a Man, my son!

Rudyard Kipling (1895)

Introduction

When My Life Changed Forever

It's 1:30 a.m. on Saturday, August 24, 1991, and I find myself naked, blindfolded, gagged, and bound in a coffin. I try to understand why I am inside a windowless van, on my way to an unknown destination.

Fifteen minutes earlier, I was coming back home after playing cards. Two well-built men jumped on me. My first reaction was to think I was being mugged. They hit me hard and I was left somewhat stunned. A few minutes later, I understood this was not a robbery as I had initially assumed. I was being kidnapped.

Less than an hour later, I am stripped to my underwear in a larger, windowless box, barely six by six feet, made of wooden board walls, in a basement, both legs chained to the floor. There is an old mattress on the floor and a blanket. I can only stretch to reach a small chemical toilet. In the corner, there's an old black-and-white TV set and a small ramshackle lamp.

I experienced the most traumatic days of my life in that place.

I spent long hours lying down, with my eyes set on a four-inch hole on the ceiling, through which my kidnappers would lower a small bag of food twice a day. Every now and then, they would replace the bag with a voice recorder and that day's newspaper so I would record the headlines and thus show I was still alive. That hole and that TV set were my only link to the outside world.

As I had seen in countless films, I was at the mercy of the good cop and the bad cop. I got the chance to hear them both. One voice would ask me time and again to stand exactly under the hole in the ceiling so he could shoot me in the head. The other one would come in the small hours. This man told me at the very beginning that to him, I would be Mario. I do not know why, but I gave him the same name. He was also Mario to me.

Conversations with Mario would go on during the night, amid a terrifying silence. His voice would reach me through that small hole in the ceiling. We discovered our shared passion for Boca Juniors. During one of our chats, I told Mario that it had been my childhood dream to be the president of Boca. When I asked him about my chances to make it out of there alive, Mario always said he would never allow anyone to kill the future president of the club.

The minute I was placed in that box, I discovered a bottle of pills next to the mattress. They told me they were sleeping pills and, as a pointless act of rebellion, I refused to take any. Every night, after talking to Mario, I would turn off the small lamp in an attempt to get some sleep. I was sure I would go crazy if I did not get any sleep, even if it was for a short while.

Upon waking, after having slept for no more than four or five hours, I would spend long intervals still, silent, and in semidarkness. I had a very strange feeling; I tried to convince myself that I was still asleep and that everything around me was part of a dream. Despite feeling the chains around my ankles, I believed that the minute the lights went on, I would be lying in my bed, in my bedroom, at home.

The newspaper headlines on August 1991 talked about the collapse of the Soviet Union; Ukraine's declaration of independence; and Carlos Menem, who had been the president for two years by then. They discussed the recent convertibility plan, which since April had established that in Argentina a peso was worth one US dollar. The local soccer scene was going through a difficult conflict over TV broadcasting rights.

During those days, I went through every imaginable emotion and state of mind. At times, I was certain they were going to kill me. I found out weeks later, that had been the outcome for seven people who had been kidnapped by the same gang of former police chiefs and oppressors who had taken part in the last military government. On TV I was able to take a peek into reality: people went about with their lives.

However, the following Thursday, everything changed and I felt the squeeze of anguish within me. On the tiny TV screen, I watched how a swarm of reporters and TV cameras were posted at my father's house in Barrio Parque. Shouting at the top of his voice, Dad tried to make himself heard by the reporters, addressing them from his balcony. In a matter of days—during which, due to safety reasons, only a handful of close people knew about my disappearance—my kidnapping had become the main headline across all media.

I was only thirty-two years old. The images of my three children and every member of my family appeared on the screen and in my mind constantly. I missed them and was afraid I would never see them again. I was overwhelmed by a strong sense of guilt because of the suffering I was causing them. Every time I saw them, my anguish would become unbearable. I was desperate about the concern I saw outside, in that place that seemed unreachable.

There, in that basement, I learned to spend long hours in silence, an old habit from Calabria that I had seen my paternal grandfather, Giorgio, practice many times during my childhood. Being kidnapped is an awful experience I do not even wish upon my worst enemy.

Amid that silence, only seldom broken by a leaking faucet, the TV static, or the hum of a passing car—I still did not know I was being held below Juan de Garay Avenue, in the Constitución neighborhood—I would dive into my thoughts. Thinking was my way of surviving captivity.

I wanted to live, but that did not depend on me. It was a decision beyond my capabilities. I would repeatedly ponder what my life would be like if I survived. By then, I was merely a "little fish," a nickname given to me by my kidnappers. To them, I was the successor, the first born, Franco Macri's heir. At that time, I worked beside my father at the helm of Sideco, his construction company.

Rather paradoxically, I suddenly started to think big, out of the box, in this case, literally. I thought that if I made it out alive, my life would change completely. I remember a conversation I had with a friend of my father's when I was fifteen. He said something that would stay with me forever:

"There will come a moment in your life when you will have to choose between being or having."

I thought about doing things that would help people live better lives. I thought of fulfilling childhood dreams. I thought that life, which doesn't give us second chances, just may grant me one. I thought about being free and independent. I thought about Boca, about the great city I lived in. I thought about Argentina and the many things that could be changed. I thought of something that I couldn't quite put a name to at the time but which I later learned was vocation for service. I, who had been given everything, thought that if I made it out alive, I might come to the point when it would be time to start giving back. Likely for the first time in my life, I had the chance to choose my future. I had found my own *what for*, my purpose.

Following the ransom payment, there was an interval without any contact with my family. I was certain my death was inevitable. At night, Mario would tell me how my captors would discuss what to do with me.

Three days went by during which I could not establish who might be feeling worse, my family or me, until one night, they decided to let me go. A voice ordered me to face away from the door and, for the first time, I heard the creaking of the box door as it opened. "You are leaving. Put this sweat suit on." It was Mario's voice and I felt his hand on my shoulder. When they set me free, in the middle of nowhere, I felt I had been reborn. The time had come to choose another life. A new life that would lead me alongside thousands, then hundreds of thousands, and finally millions of people to places that had only existed in my wildest dreams.

One never knows when you are going to find your true vocation, but if there is one thing I have learned, it is to not accept things as they are presented to us and to always be open. This is like love; it is a vibration you only feel in your heart. We should never resign ourselves to living without love or not finding our vocation. They are out there, waiting for us. It is about finding them. They are our *what for*.

This book is about the mysterious road toward happiness. It is about my personal journey and what I have learned along the way. It is the *what for* behind so many things accomplished and lived, and the many yet to be conquered. *Why* be the president of a soccer club, *why* change a city, and, above all, *why* change a country.

This is dedicated to those who worked with me during each stage and those who are now setting off on their own journeys, wherever these might take them. For all of you, here is my experience.

MAURICIO MACRI
September 2022

PART ONE

Leadership

From Sideco to Boca

1

A New Quality

Boom, boom, boom. The ball bounced against the wall of the bedroom I shared with my brother Gianfranco in the apartment overlooking Plaza Vicente López. Mom would tell me to cut it out, but I didn't listen. I kept kicking it repeatedly. I was eleven or twelve years old and I would kick the ball, or rather tried to, with my right foot, my left foot, with the inside of the foot, instep, the toe, harder, slower, trying to curve the ball inward, outward.

I suspect our neighbors must have come to our door to complain about this monotonous sound on more than one occasion. At that age, the one thing I wanted more than anything in the world was to master the technique of Boca Juniors' greatest players. Famous names such as Rojas, Madurga, Curioni, and many others whose feats I read about every week in *El Gráfico.* I dreamed of becoming a skillful number nine. As was the case with so many boys, I could just see myself climbing the fence at La Bombonera, after having scored the goal that defined the championship. I believed that in order to achieve this, the only way was through hard practice. Kicking the ball time and time again. Assessing and trying to improve, even if it only a little.

The constant ball kicking against the wall barely resulted in that boy becoming a discreet amateur player over the years. It also taught me a lesson that has stayed with me forever: Only by persisting do we accomplish our goals.

The lessons we learn as young children are those that are forever most clearly imprinted in our minds. In my case, I decided to create a soccer team along with my classmates. I went to Cardenal Newman, a Catholic school with a strong Irish tradition, where rugby was above any other sport.

My interest in creating the team was not without its purpose. I knew from the start that it was the way to secure a place in the team, given my poor skill as a player. Somehow, I learned to lead in order to be able to play. During my high school years, I was the one who put together the team, got the jerseys, looked for any tournament where we would be allowed to sign up, and called my classmates, one by one, to remind them of practice times. I devoted a sizeable portion of my time to logistics so that our soccer team would thrive. It was then that I realized I was starting to enjoy that solitary role I had set up for myself.

During my teenage years in the seventies, the school exerted considerable pressure for all its students to play rugby. The rugby tradition at Cardenal Newman gave rise to one of the most important teams in the local tournament. To be able to play, it was necessary to attend rigorous and demanding training during the week. For many, the pace was too much and, despite pressure from their families and the school, they dropped out of the activity. It did not take me long to realize that it was among those who were no longer playing rugby that I would find my pool of new soccer players.

The education we received at school was geared toward one recurring idea: the team is always above individualities. In this sense, rugby is an excellent vehicle for transmitting the Christian Brothers' philosophy. Rugby has a very clear educational function: being part of a rugby team calls for a high degree of perseverance and discipline. The scrum is a metaphor for the importance of team coordination in pursuit of a great result.

I played rugby at school despite being an even worse player with the oval ball than with the round one. I took it very seriously and trained every Tuesday and Thursday come rain or shine, in every temperature. Rugby taught me about the importance of teamwork. That idea of standing by and for one another is very strong. It means that in rugby, against all mathematical rules, one plus one may equal three.

In the meantime, my duties as the head of the soccer team kept growing. I went into every class trying to convince other students to join our team. Gathering eleven teenagers to play on Sundays was a tall order. During that stage in life, the sense of responsibility is still forming; last minute absences were frequent and, to make matters worse, the best players used to be the most irresponsible. I was always running after everything and everyone.

My dedication was explained by my desire to play on a soccer team and I quickly realized that if I did not lead the effort, there would be no soccer match. There was no other boy willing to take on the job. It was necessary for someone to roll up their sleeves and stand behind every detail. That someone, more out of necessity than anything else, ended up being me.

At twenty-one, I took a huge leap forward and faced my first big personal project. It was bold, almost absurd. In a moment of utter oblivion, I decided to organize a tour for our team in the United States! I don't exactly recall what it was that made me think we were remotely ready to take such a step; I only remember my profound conviction that something of this magnitude was feasible and my complete certainty that I would succeed.

I started sending letters to different universities around Boston to try to secure an invitation for our unknown team. To everyone's surprise, a few weeks later, we received the long-awaited invitation.

From that moment on, I threw myself into organizing every possible kind of activity to raise the money we needed to pay for the trip. I organized a festival, rented a movie theater and sold tickets for a special showing, and printed a magazine and sold advertising space. We did well and reached our target, so much so that we even had enough extra money to organize a new tour the following year, this time, to Austin, Texas.

I was the team's manager, coach, captain, and a player. Among my many tasks, there was one almost impossible to achieve: I had to somehow contain a group of unruly and wildly excited twenty-year-old boys traveling abroad together to play soccer. God knows how I managed it, but I certainly did. I was starting to discover a new and mysterious quality: I could lead.

2

A Cultural Change at Thirty

I know. One thing is to lead a group of youngsters who want to play soccer and have fun and another is to lead an organization that carries the complexities of a company.

Right after earning my engineering degree, I began to work alongside my father. Dad had started to involve me in his activities a long time before that. He enjoyed taking me to his business meetings. I would always sit by his side, barely a teenager, without really understanding what it was all about.

That was a world away from being a twenty-five-year-old who was taking his place at Sideco, the great construction company that my father started in the sixties and, at the time, was one of the most important in the country. How did I get there?

Dad was staunchly against giving me a position that carried such responsibility. In addition to this, the company was going through some difficult times. One the one hand, Sideco had accumulated great debts; on the other, the Argentine economy during the second half of the 1980s was rearing its ugly head again.

It was me who insisted on it. I wanted to prove to myself and to my father that I was able to turn Sideco around. Dad held fast as long as he could and resorted to every means at his disposal to make me change my mind. But just like Mom with the ball, he couldn't stop me. There was no doubt I would succeed.

One of the managers approached me and asked, "Why are you so intent on working at Sideco? Don't you see it is done for?" I remember my answer, "Look, I may turn it around. I hope I will, but if it does go bankrupt, I will have learned a lot." The manager stared at me in disbelief probably thinking, *This kid is insane*, but turned around and left.

Finally, and after many battles, I managed to convince Franco Macri and I arrived at Sideco. I would be in charge of the team he had had been forming over the years—a group of extraordinary engineers who had been with the company from the very beginning.

The team at Sideco knew my Dad and his leadership style well. Franco could be brilliant and, at the same time, authoritarian. He was bold and dictatorial but his exuberant charisma was above any analysis of his qualities as a leader.

My arrival at the construction company made me face a huge challenge. I knew I had some advantage as I had been appointed to the position by my father. The Sideco team had utter and unconditional admiration toward him. If he had decided I should take that position, they assumed Franco had his reasons. His aura protected me and I finally had the owner's blessing. That team had the utmost respect for the Macri last name.

Still, I could not ignore an enormous challenge. From the very beginning, I knew that comparisons between father and son would be inevitable. Faced with each decision, the same ghost, the same threat would appear. Dad had left a lasting imprint on the company he had founded and on the team that had grown alongside it.

It was neither the first nor the last time that living in my father's shadow would be a heavy burden to bear. Dad was my teacher and I admired him, but from an early age, I knew we were different. Paradoxically, that constant comparison forced me to follow my own path. I had known this since I was very young. As with all children, in order to be yourself, it is vital to build your own identity.

The idea I had been considering, which I wanted to implement at Sideco, was the result of the times during that second half of the 1980s. The economy was plummeting, a consequence of its age-old problems: high inflation, high fiscal deficit, unpayable debt, and currency instability. The nation was once again bankrupt and therefore no longer able to provide the quality public services that Argentines had received in the past. The economic model that President Raúl Alfonsín had spearheaded was on the verge of collapse. Sooner rather than later, I believed the large state-owned public service companies would be privatized and the private sector would be called upon to manage the service concessions. I decided that Sideco should be prepared for when that happened.

I remember perfectly well the moment I met with all the managers to formally tell them about the new strategic path ahead. They had all worked with my father. They looked at me somewhat condescendingly and suspiciously, as if they were thinking: "We have been a construction company for years and this young man is telling us we now need to be a service company?"

The change I was proposing was based on a simple concept: If Sideco had a been a company that had given proof, along its history, of being able to build roads, highways, industrial facilities of every kind, and hydroelectric power plants, why would it not be able to manage them? I have always maintained that it is more difficult to embark on a construction than to administer a service. The time had come to prove it.

Still, in order to succeed at this, I had to face the fears of the company's old and dear engineers. My proposal had led several to think that their lifelong work was going to lose value. My reasoning was exactly the opposite: the idea of a new strategic challenge could mean an increase in their self-esteem and an opportunity for the development of new capabilities. What was clear at that time was that the logic that had led Sideco to the position it held corresponded to another model of the country. A model that was showing signs of exhaustion. The end of an era.

This is how Sideco went from being the leading construction company in the market to becoming an important provider of public services. Those incipient ideas gave rise to great projects, such as the concession to Autopistas del Sol, the extraordinary transformation of Acceso Norte and General Paz Avenue, which surrounds the city of Buenos Aires. It was a job planned and designed from an engineering standpoint, in a completely different way from anything that had been done until then. Lanes, lighting, and accesses were expanded without ever interrupting the circulation of vehicles on their route. It was the first case in which the private sector carried out a job without receiving public funds. Financing was provided by the winning company, which would only begin to recover its investment once the work was completed, through toll collection. However, this was not the only project. The gas distributor in Córdoba and Cuyo was another success case. We also developed a highway concessionaire and a water concessionaire in Corrientes, among others.

At Sideco, I grew a lot. Above all, I began to increasingly understand what lies behind the mystery of leadership, which I had discovered when putting together the school team. In the business world, my management experience at Sideco was my first success.

It was not just about changing a strategy. I changed a corporate mentality. That young man in his early thirties had achieved, for the first time, a cultural change.

3

First Lessons

In those early days at Sideco, I made a somewhat absurd decision, stemming from my own fears. I decided to grow a mustache to appear older. The suit, the strict tie, and of course, the mustache sought to disguise my inexperience. Over the years, I knew it was silly, but at that time, it seemed like a valid resource to stand in front of those managers who were twice my age.

However, I also resorted to another resource. One that I still hold, value, and recommend to those who are beginning to take leadership positions in any field. It always works. It is about leading by example. There is no possible leadership if there is no coherence between the values that are expressed and one's personal conduct. Leading others necessitates exemplary behavior. It is the first requirement and it is unavoidable. It was the first lesson I learned when I took a leadership position.

I still found it difficult to assume the position of boss. I needed people to trust me, to believe in me. My first idea was, therefore, to work harder than everyone else, to be the first to arrive and the last to leave the office. At that time, it was a simple way to convey my commitment to the task. If you're there, I reasoned, it's because you care, it's because the goals are shared. I never understood absent bosses. Physical presence is part of leading by example.

Work culture was one of the best legacies I received from my father. When we are children, we learn from what we see in those around us. Dad was like that. When it came to him, work came above all else. He knew it was essential to roll up one's sleeves and "carry the team on one's shoulders," as they say in the world of soccer, a world that, paradoxically, Dad was not very familiar with.

But while leading by example is always necessary, it is not enough to lead teams. Before teams, there are people. You lead with very different people, personalities, ways of working and relating. Over the years, I learned to get to know people better and understand their enormous diversity.

Sometime after Sideco, I arrived at Sevel, the automaker that Dad had acquired in the early 1980s and had the license to manufacture Fiat and Peugeot cars. The automotive sector represented a real quantum leap in terms of experience after my time at the construction company. I had barely sat down in my new office when I found out that the director of purchasing and the director of production had not spoken to each other in five years. In an industrial facility, these are two positions that must function under extreme coordination and work almost like Siamese twins because the production line is supplied by the purchasing department. This is where the famous "just in time" concept comes from. According to this concept, it is essential to have the necessary parts at the exact moment, neither before nor after, to avoid shortages but also not to immobilize capital with a larger stock than strictly necessary. This calls for enormous efficiency so that the production line never stops. This was a key development for the success of the Japanese automotive industry in gaining competitiveness against its North American counterparts.

But at Sevel, I immediately discovered that exactly the opposite was happening. The two directors, of Italian origin, had decided to stop talking to each other for reasons unknown to everybody. Resolving this conflict was one of my first tasks. I remember deciding to hire the services of an international consultancy that offered a customer-centered quality program and had experience in this type of problem related to interpersonal relationships. The program lasted three days and consisted of a series of talks with the consultancy experts. I tried to see if the relationship between the two directors improved, but they continued to show indifference toward each other.

At the end of the presentations, on the last day, the organizers of the program proposed a series of recreational activities. Among them was the "three-legged race," where pairs are formed, one person's right leg is tied to the other person's left leg, and they must move forward in sync to avoid falling. Naturally, they chose the two directors who were not on speaking terms. They were mortified when they found out that they would have to do the race together. After a few yards, they fell to the ground. They laughed heartily, along with everyone else. Problem solved. From that moment on, the factory began to work in perfect harmony again, without any tension between the two and, of course, the quality standards improved greatly. That's where I discovered something that I would later use on countless occasions. The best way to resolve conflicts between people is to spend time together outside office hours, in spaces for play and fun, where you can leave the work environment behind to build stronger and more resilient relationships, reduce distance, and eliminate prejudices. Consolidating a team requires this type of shared experiences. Soccer at the Olivos presidential residence during my administration and the retreats we did with the cabinet ministers on more than one occasion are examples of this idea. Teams need to develop strong personal ties. If they don't, success is not possible.

The objective of a leader is always to bring the best out of those around them. We are not all the same, we do not all act in the same way. It took me a long time to better understand the characteristics of different types of personalities and styles.

There are those who need less pressure to fully commit to the task, and there are others who function better when pressure increases. There are those who need to be assured a leading role within a project, while others need to preserve their personal spaces. Some need to receive displays of affection that reinforce their commitment, while others prefer to work with greater detachment, without any emotional consideration. Everyone contributes in one way or another to the group project.

My own path to leadership led me to develop a psychologist's view of people. I believe, without false modesty, that it is one of my best qualities. I learned to perceive and detect the importance of different moods and their effects on daily work. I understood the importance of knowing much more about those around me then and now: their dreams, frustrations, and aspirations. I learned to search for and recognize the potential that my collaborators had in their professional development. I was able to anticipate their reactions in the face of demands and challenges. Psychoanalysis has been a great help for many years. The process of self-knowledge is also a process of knowledge about others that, far from being static, is constantly evolving.

I have always preferred to lead those who are equipped with their own inner drive. I learned to recognize them quickly. They are people who have initiative and proactivity. I like to define them as those who do not wait to ask for permission. It has always been much easier for me to hold someone back than to push them.

Even in situations where someone, due to excess action, may jeopardize a project, I learned that it is always possible to have a conversation. Sometimes you need to take a break and create the space for the other person to listen to an alternative point of view and the convenience, if necessary, of slowing down. Throughout my life, I found it better to surround myself with these restless and challenging personalities than to work with people who lack initiative or who are excessively afraid of the risks of their decisions.

Those who worked with me in the companies, at Boca, in the City of Buenos Aires, or in the national government know this because I have repeated it like a mantra: I prefer those who do ten things even if only seven turn out well over someone who can only do four, even if their result is extraordinary. The dynamic aspect has a value for me that stands above absolute perfection, which, as we know, is by nature unattainable. In fast times like the ones we live in, organizations must maintain a permanent vocation for change. This makes it vital to empower people to lose their fears when it comes to advancing reforms. Even when facing the costs of having to accept some small margin for error, I will always be in favor of doing.

However, to achieve that ideal team, it is necessary to ensure the autonomy of its members. This is a crucial aspect of leadership and one of the concepts that has undergone the most transformation in recent decades. When I started working in my father's company, the structures were much more rigid than they are today. At that time, proposing autonomy and freedom to work was something new that caused enormous resistance. Today, this concept has prevailed. Companies value the entrepreneurial attitude above any other quality. Some time ago, this idea was completely countercultural.

This less vertical and more autonomy-oriented style of leadership has now become an archetype and, at the same time, it continues to reinvent itself and generate new spin-offs. However, these new leadership versions still emphasize that same dynamic: the search for more empowerment and greater independence. Today's leadership requires new types of professionals, but also new models of leaders, more in line with the times and the rapid changes involved. It calls for a profound redefinition of roles. Personalities that were once rejected by organizations are now among the most sought-after.

I experienced the beginning of that radical transformation in company management models. When I started working at the company, the dream of any young person was still to have a long career within one organization. Their own identity was defined by the company where they aspired to work for the better part of their life. This required a huge effort to adapt to the logic of that company, which was supposed to remain stable through time. From the 1990s to the present day, companies have incorporated new visions and transformed their organizational models as the technological revolution unfolded.

If in the past it was necessary to adapt to molds, as time passed, it became necessary to break and challenge them. If at one time the entrepreneurial attitude was reserved exclusively for owners or shareholders, today it is a requirement for all members of a team. The very notion of leadership has changed and given way to more innovative and disruptive models.

All these changes found me at the right time and in the right place to incorporate and include them in my own construction as a leader. In hindsight, I cannot help but think that they prepared me for the challenges that came later.

Along my journey, I absorbed other rules that seemed destined to become a part of me. As had initially happened with exemplarity, I immediately incorporated another basic concept: respect.

There are leaders who work based on fear. It is a style that I do not share at all. In order to lead, respect for others is essential. Leading is always about giving. You have to give what you advocate. If the leader does not give, they do not lead, they force, which is something very different.

For Dad, it was common to skimp on recognition. Acknowledging effort and achievements is, first and foremost, acknowledging the other person. Many times, such acknowledgement is the greatest reward people seek. It can be material recognition, though in most cases, it's something different. Human beings seek emotional and affective recognition. To provide this, it's important to open up: open your mind and also your heart. I believe I have improved on this aspect compared to my father but I know I still have a way to go. Recognition and encouragement from someone in a leadership position toward someone who has accomplished the proposed objective is an essential tool. Giving, that is what it is all about.

The main mistake a leader can make at the beginning of their career is to lack the ability to delegate. Delegating is going against one's own narcissism. It involves ceasing to believe that only you are capable of doing things well. That illusion of feeling like the center of the universe is toxic. Isolation, surrounding yourself with people who are constantly praising you, and being removed from the second and third lines in the daily work processes are all elements that jeopardize any leadership project.

I always sought and enjoyed talking with those who do not sit on the boards but are closer to the day-to-day operation of any activity. When I undertook the great reconversion of Sideco, my first allies were the younger executives. When we talked, I allowed myself to use a different, more direct language. The older executives needed more time and more trust to be able to release the handbrake. The young ones had quickly understood my message and were eager to start changing things right away. The same thing would happen to me in Boca and later in politics.

In that moment when I had to turn a company around at such a young age, I discovered a characteristic of change that has stayed with me in everything I have undertaken later: Change always grows from the bottom up. The leader is just an interpreter. He is someone who expresses that collective will to make things different. However, change cannot be forcefully imposed. On the contrary, it matures and grows; oftentimes, progress is not linear and it always presents advances and setbacks.

People always come first. The Sideco engineers were the ones who dared to take a chance. The Boca partners were the ones who believed that the time had come to transform a stagnant institution into a modern and successful club. The residents of the city of Buenos Aires were the ones who decided to bet on something new. And the citizens were the ones who decided, through their vote in 2015, that it was finally time to try to change the culture of power in Argentina.

After my kidnapping, after my experience in Sideco, and after my time at Sevel, I felt prepared to fulfill a new goal, but there was a problem. In order to achieve it, I had to take a decisive step: to become independent from my father.

I had set a monumental objective for myself, the most important one that any human being can have: I had decided no less than to fulfill a childhood dream.

4

What Do You Want to Be When You Grow Up?

I am not quite sure how Boca entered my life. It's true that my Dad was a Boca fan. It was to be expected from a barely nineteen-year-old Italian immigrant who arrived in Argentina in 1949. However, soccer was far from being the center of his life; he would get bored at the stadium. I've been a Boca fan for as long as I can remember. I have no idea where my passion for soccer came from. I have no explanation for its origin. It's been with me forever.

I had two dreams. I have already mentioned the first one: to be the best number nine in Boca's history. A natural scorer, an idol to the fans. But I had another dream parallel to that: to be the president of Boca. Of course, I had not the slightest idea what being the president of Boca meant. I was not in a position to imagine what he did or how he spent his time, that is, what his job entailed.

Notwithstanding, I wanted to be the president of Boca. I think it may have had to do with the fact that my father knew Alberto J. Armando, the legendary president of the club between 1960 and 1980. At that time, my father and Armando had partnered in an insurance company.

Armando was a figure who was present at home and my father often mentioned his name.

In the early 1970s, the president of Boca had launched a very ambitious project: the construction of a new stadium on the grounds of Ciudad Deportiva, on a huge plot of land reclaimed from the river in the Costanera Sur area of the city. My Dad was hired by Boca and oversaw the installing of the hundreds of piles that would be the base of the stadium for over one hundred thousand spectators that Armando had promised to open on May 25, 1975. I still remember a photo of me from those times, with my head covered by a helmet, accompanying my father and Armando on the construction site. To my delight, and as part of his payment, the president of the club promised to give my Dad two boxes in the new stadium.

Armando was an extraordinary salesman. The stadium was never built, and the cutting-edge development at Ciudad Deportiva was never completed. It is possible that the figure of Alberto Jota, as we called him at home, inspired my dream. I don't know. In any case, at ten or eleven years old, when some adult asked me the classic question, "Mauricio, what do you want to be when you grow up?" I would confidently and firmly reply in all seriousness, "I'm going to be the president of Boca."

Many years passed since that childhood dream. For me, the path to the club was quite simply the path to independence. After the kidnapping, the relationship with my father became stormy. I had long concluded that to be myself, I had to distance myself from him.

I don't remember the exact date, but it must have happened around 1987. One day Pedro Pompilio, who was the club's treasurer at the time, came to see me at my office. Boca was going through a terrible financial situation and he wanted to know if I would be willing to help. The situation was dire, Boca was bankrupt and needed urgent money to clean up its accounts. I helped with the purchase of Walter Perazzo and some other players and managed to get Sevel to support the club by having the Fiat brand on its jersey.

A few years later, a group of members invited me to participate in the ticket headed by Antonio Alegre and Carlos Heller. They explained their ideas to me for a while, we discussed the problems the institution was facing, and at the end of the meeting, they asked me if I would be willing to join their ticket, fully assuming I would accept. Some were already getting up to leave when I announced, "Thank you, gentlemen, for the invitation, but maybe some other time. I wanted to tell you that I have decided to run for the presidency of the club in the next election, at the end of '95." They all looked at me with the same surprised and somewhat compassionate look that adults gave me as a child when they heard me say that I was going to be president of Boca. A few muttered, "I hope so," and others seemed to be in the presence of an alien. It was 1991. I had said no to them.

Antonio Alegre was a good person. Together with Carlos Heller, they drove Boca through a strange ideological alliance between a conservative strongman and a communist banker. Together, they led the club downhill. From the office I still had at Socma, I began to call various friends who were fans of Boca, friends of friends, acquaintances, and others to ask them if they would be willing to join the project that was taking shape in my head. What happened took me by surprise. It was an overwhelming response.

I discovered a rare and novel phenomenon. Something that for unknown reasons would happen to me many times once I entered politics. Every time I spoke about my willingness to participate, it was as if I released a current of commitment onto others. Many approached me after hearing my story and told me that, indeed, perhaps the time had come, that if I had the courage, why couldn't they also do it? It was a shock wave that showed the desire to be a part of changing things and to accompany me along the path I proposed.

I remember the meetings with Pedro Pompilio, Luis Conde, José Cirilo, and Jorge Bitar, among others. They were different people from those I was used to in the business world. Some were true characters, veterans of Boca's leadership teams. On one hand, our opponents had done a good job in rescuing a club that was literally bankrupt: they had managed to revive it. However, despite the effort made, Alegre and Heller lacked a long-term strategy, they had not managed to organize the club, and Boca lacked a competitive soccer team.

The first electoral campaign of my life now lay ahead of me. I visited every neighborhood of the city and the suburbs holding small events. It was decisive for us that the active members, the only ones authorized to vote, massively mobilized on the day of the election. Our only source of information was an old photocopy of the members' registry. We started calling them one by one to tell them about our proposal and invite them to our meetings. We had created a slogan: "Go back to our glory days."

The idea of the lost glory led me to call upon those who had been the best representatives of that past: the players who had worn the jersey and had lifted trophies. They had to become my best advisors. I wanted to have them close and listen to them. Each one had the irreplaceable value of their experience. It was essential to have them on board from day one, if I happened to win the elections, of course.

They were illustrious names: Rattín, Tano Roma, Marzolini, Rojas, and many more. I had admired them on the pitch, and surrounding myself with them brought me an enormous sense of security. They helped us to attract more and more fans willing to participate in the change and to recover that enormous history that had fallen into a pit of decadence.

I confess that at first my speech was somewhat aggressive and daring. I spoke of ending the "unmentionables," as I would call the people of River Plate, our historic rival. At the same time, I announced the end of their sporting hegemony, as under the guidance of their coach, Ramón Díaz, they were winning everything. I went as far as to promise that Boca would win a championship every year and that our club would be recognized as one of the most important in the world. It was no small feat.

I was all intuition. I sought to represent the feelings of the Boca fan. I wanted to channel those tens of thousands of members who seemed to desire a new prominence.

I knew I was putting an enormous amount of pressure on myself. However, those goals that seemed unattainable were achieved, and at the end of my entire experience in Boca, we had won more than one tournament per year. Seventeen in twelve years to be exact.

Leadership always starts with a first task: to have a dream. It doesn't matter if it seems utopian and unachievable; what matters is getting thousands of people behind it and then, together, working to make it a reality. What sets a dreamer apart from a leader lies precisely in that aspect. The dreamer does not need others and does not have the commitment to make their dream a reality. The leader does.

In Boca, I had an additional challenge. My entire professional training and experience had been built in my father's large companies. Our electoral campaign was based on passion and enthusiasm. We lacked the type of organization we badly needed. Despite the willingness and enthusiasm shown by people like Gregorio "Goyo" Zidar, Orlando Salvestrini, Carlos Bottaro, Julio Ramos, and Osvaldo Cabano, among many others, the scale seemed overwhelming. We had to establish work systems, share responsibilities, generate meetings with members, and develop a very long list of logistical tasks. We needed to share our proposals in specialized media. Club politics also found a place: we had to seek alliances with groups that were more sympathetic to the idea of the new Boca that we were trying to spread.

It was not easy to communicate what we wanted to do. At the time, Torneos y Competencias had a huge influence among sports media. Carlos Avila's business had the television broadcasting rights for soccer and he personally had a strong affinity for Alegre and Heller's administration. Fortunately, Gerardo Sofovich, the unforgettable producer and Boca fan, shared our *what for*. His program, *Tribuna Caliente,* gave me the opportunity to have a spot on TV from which I could communicate directly with the fans.

From then on, I understood a concept that had a huge impact on my way of understanding communication and it comes from the logic of judo. In judo, strength comes from the opponent, not from oneself. I discovered that the more outraged Heller became with my candidacy and the more aggressive he was toward me, the more sympathy I received from the Boca fans. Since then, the aggression and attacks on the part of my rivals have always become a very important component of my strength.

I needed my project to be disruptive. I wanted to make it clear that my presidency would not be more of the same. I was searching for something that would symbolize the beginning of a new stage. It had to be something physical, something that could be seen, touched, and experienced. Passion becomes abstract if it is not embodied in something concrete. My engineer's reasoning prevailed, and the idea of rebuilding the stadium and turning it into a new Bombonera emerged. It was time to transform the physical place of glory and bring it up to date.

Those of us who have decided to participate publicly know that inevitably there are personal costs that must be faced. In my case, my rivals unleashed a huge number of messages aimed at disqualifying me. I had already experienced my father's stigmatization, in his role as a businessman, launched by some politicians and journalists. However, now it was me who had decided to expose myself to prejudices and lies. "The little prince," "the rich kid," "Daddy's boy," "the inexperienced young man who's not streetwise," those were just some of the phrases they used to try to weaken me. The negative burden of resentment and underestimation taught me to always remain centered. Not responding, not paying attention, not returning personal attacks requires profound learning. That first electoral campaign also helped me to grow.

Alegre and Heller had marked the year 1995 with two events of enormous impact on the people of Boca: the arrival of a historic Boca figure, Silvio Marzolini as coach and the return of Diego Maradona to the team. Along with him, the arrival of Kily González, Claudio Caniggia, and Darío Scotto was announced.

Finally, it was Sunday, December 3. Boca Juniors was leading the league table and had a tough match ahead against Racing Club de Avellaneda. I was overcome by anxiety. I still knew nothing in the morning. It was only after midday that I started to feel something was changing. Exit polls told us we were close, but nobody dared to confirm a result. I paced up and down. There was nothing left to do but wait.

That afternoon ten goals were scored at La Bombonera. Six for Racing and four for Boca. And I won my first election. It was a double thrill. I had led a new project and, at the same time, I was fulfilling my oldest dream. It was also the triumph of the people over prejudices. It was the triumph of change over the status quo. I didn't know that a wonderful decade lay ahead. How could I have known? Still, I was sure that I was about to embark on the most incredible journey of my life. I had found my *what for*.

A few days after the elections, my cell phone rang. It was the mother of a classmate from school. She had asked her son for my number because she wanted to tell me something. She said, "Mauricio, you may not remember, but when you were eleven years old, you came over for a playdate one afternoon and told me that when you grew up, you were going to be the president of Boca."

5

Between Dreams and Reality

I experienced firsthand that idea of leadership as a shared dream during my time as president of Boca. Toward the end of 1995, I became aware that the second chapter of my story was beginning. The first part concluded on election day Sunday. It was time to turn my dream, which was no longer just mine but belonged to many people, into a reality.

I felt the support of thousands of members and the displays of support and affection I received multiplied. But when I got home after the first few days leading the club and managed to be alone for a while, a very strong feeling emerged: responsibility.

I had managed to make them believe in me and follow me. My responsibility was to give back everything I had received by fulfilling my promises. I sensed, rightly, that from that moment on I would be under a relentless scrutiny. The eyes of millions of Boca fans across the country were now on me. It was a new world. Like at Sideco and Sevel, I felt the obligation to live up to what I had myself generated.

Each of my plans and projects would depend on a single thing to become a reality. I had to satisfy the urgent aspirations of Boca's fans, aspirations that can be summed up in a single word that has magical powers in the soccer world: winning. However, I knew that sporting results were at risk of being delayed. I have always believed, and Boca reaffirmed this for me, that institutions come first. In order to have positive results, a solid institutional foundation is needed. It is from that strength, even in a soccer club, that a spirit of change is born. Without that spirit, it is impossible to achieve success.

My urgency was different from that of the fans. My campaign proposals included ideas that carried a strong symbolic component and could be implemented quickly. That's how I decided to propose a renovation and upgrade of our stadium. The work would take six months and allow me to gain the necessary time to carry out the changes that were needed as well as consolidate my authority. I would bring to the television studios a mockup of how the Bombonera would look once renovated.

Architect Carlos Sallaberry, from Justo Solsona's firm, who had been responsible for designing the World Cup stadium in Mendoza, proposed to me to renovate the old box seats area, eliminate the old moat that separated the pitch from the stands, build press work areas (something unheard of in Argentina at the time), and rebuild bathrooms and other facilities to have a stadium that lived up to Boca's mystique.

It was a key decision because it meant moving from words to action. I decided to face the costs of the architectural project out of my own pocket. I was in a hurry and my anxiety led me to do something that was at the limits of what was allowed by the club's internal regulations.

Finally, I rented a bulldozer and, for the first time in my life, I climbed up to drive it myself. I aimed at the old boxes that faced Del Valle Iberlucea Street. That's how the demolition began. However, I had a problem: I had overlooked the fact that the assembly of members had not yet met to approve the reform that was already tendered and underway. I had no alternative. I felt the urgency to show results and knew that the job would take months.

I had started my administration in the last days of 1995 and wanted to finish the renovation by April 3, 1996, so that we could reopen the stadium on the anniversary of the club's founding. When the assembly of members was finally held, there were no major problems and the job was approved with broad support. There was one exception. A woman, Dr. Estela Iribarren, if I remember correctly, the only woman who had active participation in the institutional life of the club at that time, stood up and gave me a stern and angry look. She said, "Mr. Macri, you ask us to approve the construction of a new stand but the old stand is no longer there. What alternative do I have?"

Due to my enthusiasm and eagerness to take action, I had crossed a line. At the end of the assembly, I approached her and offered my apologies. I knew she had a point. I explained to her what my motivations had been and we ended up talking for a long time. I felt that we had both been able to listen to and understand each other. Many years later, that woman became an important support when I moved on to the govern the City of Buenos Aires. That day, we agreed that we would officially inaugurate the new boxes together once the job was completed.

My second major symbolic act had to do with another campaign promise. I had proposed that Boca should recover its youth divisions. I was convinced that a good part of the necessary identity for the change we were seeking was in the kids who were starting to play and stand out as athletes. On the road to recovering the mystique, I wanted to make the fans identify with the stories of players who had emerged from the club itself. However, to achieve this objective, we had to modernize the structure of the youth divisions, update the working method, the practice sessions, and above all, the joint education and sports training. We built state-of-the-art facilities for the kids at Casa Amarilla. As a result, the youngest players, who lived and trained at the club, began to develop a strong sense of belonging.

My bet in this regard had a full name. I had promised to hire Jorge Griffa to lead the club's youth divisions. Actually, I had hired Griffa before the elections because I didn't want to lose him. I had committed to pay him a year's salary out of my own pocket if I was defeated. Given his experience and track record in leading countless young boys, Griffa was the right person to head the project I had in mind.

Both symbols, the stadium refurbishment and the hiring of Griffa to lead the youth teams, meant taking big risks. The relationship between leadership and risk is a topic that I will come back to on more than one occasion. There is no leadership without risk. In other words, there is no insurance that a leader can take to avoid uncertainty. However, these risks that I took had a very clear meaning. I wanted them to become a message for all those who had supported us through their vote: I wanted to convey that everything we were doing was serious and that there would be no turning back.

The financial situation caused by the commitments inherited from the previous administration made work very difficult from day one. The control that Carlos Heller had held over the club in the last part of his mandate had disastrous effects, particularly in the relationship between the players and the club.

Heller had instilled a curious ideological conception in the team. He had deceived the players into believing that Boca was a kind of gigantic cooperative that made them shareholders of the club, a notion far removed from their status as hired employees.

Shortly after my arrival, a strong crisis erupted within the professional team. I had to redefine the payments that players received for playing the summer friendly matches. The long years of disorder had taken their toll, priorities had been altered, and the accounts didn't add up at all. In this sense, the summer of 1996 was unforgettable because it brought about the first of a series of lessons that were vital for what would come later.

The meeting was held in Mar del Plata. It started after dinner and ended shortly before dawn, after hours of discussions. Mono Navarro Montoya, Colorado Mac Allister, Gamboa, Fabri, and Carrizo were there. The players made a payment demand that was impossible to satisfy.

They demanded nothing less than half of all of Boca's income from friendlies. Not only was this far removed from the club's economic possibilities, but it was also an irrational request.

The story had its origin in Carlos Heller's irresponsibility. In a display of demagogy, the former vice president, had repeatedly told the players for years that the club belonged to them. And in the height of madness, he had assured them that the money they received as payment for playing represented the same 50 percent that they were now demanding from me in Mar del Plata. The leaders of the players' protest expressed themselves as if they were owners or at least co-owners of Club Atlético Boca Juniors. Therefore, they felt that they had the necessary authority to tell me that their power was above that of the coach or the president elected by sixty percent of the club members.

The argument was getting heated. I tried to explain that Heller had lied to them, that their income represented only 25 percent of the total club's income. It was half of what he had assured them. I looked each one in the eye and said, "Not only did Heller lie to you. I want to make one thing clear: it will be impossible for Boca to uphold that twenty-five percent." They responded insisting on the idea that they were the true symbols of Boca. I remember standing my ground and telling them that they were mistaken. That Boca would continue to be Boca with or without them, that they were employees and not club members and that Boca's primary responsibility was to its history and not to its people.

It was a very tough meeting. But it was another sign for those who were willing to accompany the process we had recently started. It was my way of explicitly stating why I was there. Additionally, it was a way of clarifying what priorities we would have to share going forward to achieve what we had committed to do.

The question about this *what for* extends to another very similar one: *who for*. Who does the president of Boca work for? I asked myself that question several times and always found the same answer. My responsibility was to the members and the institution. It was not, despite my own fan status, to the star players on the team. If I understood that my responsibility was to satisfy the players' will, no matter how legitimate it seemed at first glance, my leadership would crumble like a sandcastle on the beach. And it would happen much faster if the club went bankrupt due to giving in to demagoguery.

Once again, I found myself reflecting on the issue of cultural change. The transformations in Boca, as well as those in the City of Buenos Aires and the nation, were not only about infrastructure improvements, institutional reforms, and the greater well-being of fans, neighbors, or citizens. I began to realize that there was something beyond that. Something that had a larger and more complex dimension. It was the first time in many years that Boca had a president who put the club's administrative and economic order ahead of the fans' idolization of the players.

The cultural change that I was proposing was much more difficult than renovating a stadium or giving greater prominence to the youth teams. It required revamping the way we faced resistance. Transforming the culture of a community, whether it is that of a company, a club, a city, or a country, is extremely difficult and demands processes that take a lot of time.

Conflicts over contracts and bonuses led us to have to do without some important figures, such as Mono Navarro Montoya and Mac Allister. Years later, when we found ourselves defending the same ideas, I called on Colo Mac Allister to join the government team as Secretary of Sports. With the same conviction with which he defended himself at Boca, he told me that over time he had come to understand that my position that summer had been the right one.

The world of soccer, in so many ways so similar to other worlds that I would come to know later, led me to take a very strong stand against political correctness and everything that was taken for granted, from the unspoken assumptions to what was accepted without question. I allowed myself to distrust the dogmas that Argentine soccer had built and turned into false truths that seemed irrefutable. I wanted to show the absurdity of overvaluing players' bonuses for their results, and I even declared that winning a championship was a bad deal for Boca.

I had decided to challenge the traditional universe of soccer and the logic that had led to its decline. The payment of bonuses every time Boca won a title destroyed the club's finances. Year after year, the solution was to take on debt or sell some valuable player so that the other players could collect their bonuses. I proposed different alternatives to solve this issue, mainly through increases in the payments that clubs receive for the broadcasting rights of the matches. However, I couldn't get the necessary support to change this system and had to learn to live with it.

There's nothing that we soccer fans like more than seeing our team win tournaments, celebrate championships, and lift trophies. It's the most visible side of soccer, the one that sells the most in the media. However, going against practically the entire leadership, I was determined to incorporate economic and financial dimensions into my administration. Soccer leaders, like those in politics, as well as fans and many journalists, frequently choose not to see the hidden costs behind the irresponsible financial decisions made with other people's money.

In this sense, the process of recovering the glory also included a tough battle for the reform of the club's statute. I'm proud to have fought for this and to have finally succeeded in making Boca's leaders take responsibility with their personal assets for the decisions they made with the institution's money. Looking back, I find that it was something revolutionary given Argentine soccer's low standards.

It took a lot of craziness to impose this criterion. I was accused of being elitist, of wanting only people with large fortunes to be able to be part of the club's leadership. The contrary is actually true: everyone can participate. Everyone who decides to be a part of the leadership through their vote in the assembly of members, in the board of directors, and even the president must be held accountable. After the judicial challenge imposed by Heller's supporters, we were successful.

To make Boca a hegemonic club, just as I had promised, I started planning its development with a long-term vision. I had to generate a change in the club that would allow us to look beyond the following Sunday. Little by little, an idea began to take shape. It was another revolution: the creation of an investment fund aimed at financing the renewal of the team. The model originated in ultra-professionalized sports in the United States.

The fund, which started trading under the strange acronym BoJuF, went public in September 1997 with securities worth $100. Among the subscribers were investors of all levels, from those who participated with one or two thousand dollars, to million-dollar investments. Together they totaled more than a thousand Boca fans interested in being part of the team's growth. In one week, the fund reached an endowment of more than $12.5 million. Of course, like any innovative initiative, it brought with it a series of unfounded criticisms and new, crazy prejudices.

The work around the fund was a fascinating journey that took months, during which we had to convince the club's leaders individually. It was time to leave behind the old logic of alliances between clubs and player representatives that was typical of Argentine soccer at that time. Unfortunately, it is still the case. To this day, transparency is still missing. It is not a coincidence that this lack of transparency is driven by many of those who oppose the transformation of clubs into sports corporations. It is a strange case because a good part of soccer is already privatized through these unclear relationships established by leaders, which are a product of the clubs poor management.

The resistance was very strong. The image of corruption that the soccer leadership had earned over the years was huge. I made a drastic decision to make everything clear from the very beginning. I myself endorsed the fund with my personal assets. I knew it was a necessary step to achieve everyone's acceptance. I did it convinced that we were on a path that deserved to be taken.

To comply with all the required laws and procedures, we had to present our idea to the authorities of the National Securities Commission. To this day, I believe they had never heard anything like it before. Their surprised faces said it all. From the present perspective, it seems incredible but in 1990s Argentina, the idea of creating an investment fund for the purchase of soccer players was pioneering and, why not, also risky.

It was another sign that things were changing. The fans accepted the project. It was a firm step that allowed me to confirm that we were on the right path. The fund was a success and ended up being profitable for those who invested their money in it. In turn, it made it possible for us to bring in players of importance, such as Martín Palermo and Guillermo Barros Schelotto, among others.

The work of a leader is not just about managing finances. Innovation plays a vital role. We decided to break the rules when we started working with Nike on the new jersey designs. When we presented that version with the yellow stripe separated from the blue by two small white lines, some fans almost had a heart attack. However, the modifications we made to the team's clothing generated more and more passion from the fans, especially the younger ones, who discovered that Boca was now a modern club with a contemporary spirit. The contrast with the aged image that Boca had when we arrived could not have been greater. The result only deepened the cycle. One innovation leads to another, and the conservatism that characterized soccer began to give way to change.

All these transformations not only changed Boca, they also changed me. They gave me certainty about the strength of what we had set in motion. Looking back, those years at Boca represented my first full-fledged battles against populism, that system that comfortably inhabits both the world of soccer and politics.

The Argentine idea of spending more than one can afford, of only thinking in the short term, of accepting what is politically correct, continues to lead many immensely popular clubs to bankruptcy. This led me to propose austerity and financial prudence as a golden rule.

I had fought hard against the idea of making decisions based solely on the emotions of fans, leaders, and even players. I discovered that blind following carries visible costs and others that take time to appear and remain hidden until they become painfully evident.

There is a dimension in which the leader's path is made with people by their side, pushing together. However, at the same time, there is another dimension where the path is traveled alone. There were very few of us who dared to modify something that had a high degree of acceptance in soccer, such as the role of professional players within the organization.

Affecting the interests of the players resulted in problems. Among other consequences, it earned me some ironic nicknames such as “Cartonero Báez,” which Diego Maradona gave me, referring to the humble witness of the death of Alicia Muñiz, Carlos Monzón’s partner. I know my image was unlikable for some. However, there were also those who saw my behavior as a change that deserved support and committed themselves even more.

For a good part of the microworld of soccer, my entrepreneurial background was perceived as an irreparable flaw. Many of the critics at that time accused me of treating Boca as if it were a business. I knew and I know all too well that Boca is not a business but arithmetic is the same in business, soccer, or politics. The goals are different, the work methodology, and access are also different. In any activity, austerity is a basic principle. It is essential to help dreams leave your mind and start to become a reality.

6

Reason and Passion

In the mid-1990s, Boca Juniors had lost much of its legendary sporting mystique. Being a Boca fan evoked a deep sense of nostalgia for a past that seemed irreversibly left behind. The attributes of the Boca sentiment were still alive: that overwhelming and passionate dimension based on devotion and dedication, the intangible elements that make up the Xeneize identity.

However, all that body of emotions couldn't be channeled in an organic way. A few months after my arrival as the president of the club, it still seemed to me that I was on a minefield where a new bomb was ready to go off every day.

Passion is a necessary energy that isn't enough for transformation. It doesn't produce results on its own. If an organization isn't built to contain it and make it productive, passion is just a waste of energy.

I had arrived with many years of accumulated business experience. I had witnessed and been a protagonist of important changes in management models for organizations. I had participated in countless meetings where we had discussed new roles, the modernization of management structures, and the transformation of assessment and decision-making systems.

But Boca was light years away from all that. Soccer clubs, like many other sectors of civil society, did not have professional leadership. Among those who accompanied me, there were people whose identity as Boca fans was indisputable, passionate people who lived their connection to the club with total fervor. But in terms of management, everything that happened in Boca was based on improvisation.

Similar to what happened with the players, many directors also saw themselves as owners of Boca. Some used the stadium as a children's party venue, celebrating their kids' birthdays with penalty tournaments on the pitch. Others deviated from their responsibilities to spend time with the players, argue with the coach, enter the locker room, take pictures with the team's stars, and accompany them on trips to the provinces or, even better, abroad. At the end of the day, the culture of soccer seemed to turn directors into children. The ideas for which we had fought so hard during the electoral campaign seemed to have been forgotten very quickly. Rationality surrendered to the condition of being a fan that every director carries inside, many of them brilliant executives or businessmen in their professional lives. Soccer and its overwhelming madness transformed them.

Boca was the place where I learned that true change is always a cultural change. It wasn't just about ideas or projects. In Boca, in the City of Buenos Aires, and in the nation, I had to face similar situations. Time and again, no matter where I went, changing the culture of power was my challenge.

I had the support and participation of some people from the corporate world. They had joined my adventure and had become part of the board of directors of the club along with other traditional leaders who had been there for a long time. Despite having different origins and trajectories, the old and the modern merged with the old culture of Argentine soccer.

I quickly discovered that the forces of the status quo always tend to neutralize the will for change. I remember that Boca had a general manager, responsible for operational management. The poor man lived under pressure, receiving contradictory orders and requests for personal favors. In the board of directors, no one seemed to understand the strategic importance of that area. My vision was completely contrary to theirs. The authority of the general manager was key in the day-to-day operations of the club. By ignoring his role, the whole organization was being jeopardized. In one of the first board meetings we had after I took over the presidency of the club, I said: "Gentlemen, you have every right to fire the general manager. You can do it whenever you want, and it depends solely on your decision. But in between each board of directors meetings, the general manager is in charge, and his authority must be respected. It is not possible for each director to think they can give orders according to their personal criteria and contradict the general manager on a daily basis. This will lead to chaos."

I had to undertake a lot of teaching and pedagogy for them to begin to understand the importance of the role of that general manager, who worked at the club and had been appointed by the administration that preceded me. As soon as I took over the presidency, the general manager presented me with his resignation. I didn't know him; I had never exchanged a word with him. I told him that I didn't understand the reasons why he wanted to leave when we hadn't even started working yet. He replied that it seemed logical to him to present his resignation since he had been appointed to the position by the outgoing president, Antonio Alegre,

"I don't understand. Are you Antonio Alegre's manager or the manager of Club Atlético Boca Juniors?" I asked bluntly. Surprised by my question, the manager responded with great pride, "Engineer, I am Boca's general manager!" Then I asked him to stop all that nonsense. His only loyalty had to be to Boca. He understood it and from that day on, I worked with him and dedicated myself fully to empowering him in front of the other leaders.

The first lesson was right before my eyes. At Boca, it was necessary to change the culture. No organization functions without accountability, processes, and tracking progress. My own experience taught me that if I couldn't change the institution's logic, my chances of success would be minimal. It was very clear to me that the management of the club should be reserved for professionals and be subject to previously agreed-upon objectives.

A year into my presidency, I realized I was making a mistake. I thought I had found relief from the four or five executives who questioned and pressured me the most. I tried to appease them by inviting them to travel with the team. After all, nothing attracts soccer executives—and their inner fans—more than being able to share the intimacy of being with the players on planes and in hotels. However, I recognized a flaw in my role as a leader. Not only did I fail to contain the rebels, but I also created a system that was profoundly unfair to those who worked quietly and with a lower profile. One day, I became aware of the great injustice my decision had caused. Everyone had the same right to travel with the team. I devised a rotating system so that nobody would be left out of the trips. The affected parties were outraged but the rest celebrated that I had appealed to another key dimension of leadership: justice and fairness. There is no healthy leadership without evenhandedness in the administration of rewards and punishments.

I had developed my own work system and was gradually implementing it in the club. From Monday to Friday, it was based on reason. On Sundays, it was driven by passion. It sounds simple, but it was no easy feat. The situation was chaotic. Everyone wanted to do everything, and everyone wanted to make decisions that resulted in discrediting one another.

I maintained the same principle that I had implemented at Sideco. I arrived at the club at eight in the morning and spent long hours there, until well into the night. At first, and despite the huge differences, I found myself living the same situation that I had experienced with that Cardinal Newman team. Once again, I was doing everything: I was the president, but I was also responsible for soccer, cleanliness, social action, and in charge of construction jobs and budgetary control. It was more than a full-time job; it was a full-life job. I enjoyed it, but it also made me suffer. As the months passed, I put all my effort into professionalizing each of the club's management areas to finally recover the role of president for which I had been elected. Professionalizing the structure was the only way to turn Boca into a modern and efficient organization.

One of my commitments during the campaign, along with the goal of winning a championship every year, was to make Boca a hegemonic club in Argentina and one of the five most important soccer clubs in the world. There was no way to achieve such a goal without learning from what the great international teams had done and were doing.

I inherited this global vision from my father. Dad traveled the world repeatedly, looking for the most suitable partners for each project. I learned from him that integration with the world is what generates growth and progress. It's not a theoretical issue. It's practical. Isolation only leads to failure.

To achieve this, we had to push the limits of both passion and rationality. We had promised to recover the lost glory. But what does glory represent? It is something intangible, immaterial, impossible to capture. It is a component that has to do with mystique. We know when there is mystique and when there is not. It cannot be bought readymade. Simple willpower is not enough to achieve it.

Paradoxically, more passion and more rationality were needed. In soccer, the emotional component is often described as "feeling passion for the jersey." When this happens, there are no big or small teams. It is that moment when strategy and tactics become insufficient. It is not exclusive to sports. It is a concept that I have experienced in the different fields where I have played a role. It is also present in business and politics. For a leader, it is fundamental. The difference is achieved through ideas and emotions. I know many excellent managers who have all the academic and technical resources required for a leadership position. But if that phenomenon of feeling passion for the jersey is not there, the project, the collective dream, the *what for*, will never turn out well.

For the leader, it is a central part of their job. They are the ones who must unite the passion for doing with the rationality of doing the right thing. Both vectors come together through their leadership. These are the most accurate indicators of the leader's degree of commitment to what they demand from those who accompany them. The leader, ultimately, has two responsibilities: one, to communicate ideas; and the other, which is nondelegable, is to transmit emotions.

7

Looking Beyond the Present

"Patience!" replied Carlos Bilardo when I asked him what we needed to quickly refine the squad and have a competitive team. In 1996, Bilardo had enough credentials to lead Boca after his performance with the Argentine national team in the World Cups of 1986 and 1990.

Time, both in soccer and politics, is always a scarce resource. However, I decided to accept the advice of the experienced coach and committed myself to obtaining the two reinforcements he had asked me to add to the team: José Basualdo and Juan Sebastián Verón.

Prioritizing and sequencing transformations is a central aspect of any process of change. It is the only way to avoid chaos and is also an extremely delicate challenge. Changing Boca meant changing its infrastructure and team. The first was within my power to attempt. For the second, I had no choice but to follow Carlos's advice.

Bilardo spelled it out, "Look, Mauricio, it's a long way off. Five will have to go and another five will come in. Another five will leave and new ones will come in, and so on… And in four or five years there will be a competitive team." I was stunned. Four or five years was too long a period of time for Argentine soccer.

I decided to control my anxiety and focus on generating the resources that would be essential to carry out the transformations. To add value to the new Boca, we needed to make a huge effort in communication and attract new sponsors willing to associate their brands with our project.

We had a spectacular start with the auction of the new VIP boxes and corporate client seats, both of which were still unfinished. It was completely unprecedented. I stood in front of a lectern with the auctioneer's hammer and generated the sales of each of the boxes, thus managing to triple the income we had expected. I raised a sum for the club that was far above what we needed to finish the new section. With that surplus, I was able to build the new facilities for the youth team in Casa Amarilla. I always liked the role of auctioneer. Until then, I had not gone beyond being the auctioneer in La Subasta *(The Auction)*, a card game that we used to enjoy at get-togethers with family and friends.

Looking back, the image of a club president leading an auction, broadcast live on television and surrounded by businessmen and celebrities, seems strange. There was a transgressive and innovative quality that clearly conveyed that something different was beginning to become a reality at Boca.

These changes in how we communicated yielded quick results. Nike was among the first companies to perceive the change and increased the value of its contract by 60 percent in exchange for Boca wearing its brand on the jersey. The

Quilmes company decided to join us with its name on the jersey, with a much higher amount than the contribution made by Parmalat. Meanwhile, Coca-Cola also supported us by doubling its contribution.

The soccer business had changed radically in Europe and we dedicated ourselves to analyzing the most relevant transformations with the goal of incorporating these new practices. In this way, we were able to initiate developments that showed us the enormous opportunity that came hand-in-hand with merchandising. Clubs are also brands loaded with values and identity. Boca immediately led the professional management of its brand, generating new income. The official Boca brand became part of the daily life of Argentines in countless mass consumption products that wanted to associate themselves with the project we were undertaking.

It's something I never tire of saying. We communicated a new idea and achieved results. Prejudices were left behind as innovation prevailed over the obsolete management model. Even when the club had not yet achieved the desired sporting results, it was a huge learning experience. The series of changes we were making, such as renegotiating bonuses, bringing in new sponsors, and developing licenses to use the club's brand and symbols, allowed us to turn around the deficit inherited from our predecessors. This made it possible for the club to strengthen and have the necessary funds to responsibly finance its projects.

There was an even bolder bet: the purchase of young players. Once again, it was something that had never been done before. When I look back on that learning curve,

I realize time and again that my main rival has never been another leader. My main opponent has always been and continues to be the status quo. It is that visceral enemy that places itself within oneself, that surrounds and envelops you with a conservative message. Why change, why take risks, why do what has never been done before, why go against routine? That all has a name: fear.

The idea of hiring young players sparked controversy and debate but I was convinced it was the way to go. The arrival of these young players, many of whom would later become undisputed stars, presented an unbeatable opportunity. So, names that would make history at Boca joined us, such as Ruiz, La Paglia, Coloccini, Moreno, Samuel, and, above all, Tévez and Riquelme. Undoubtedly, we would have to wait for the development of their talent: no one or nothing guaranteed that a teenager who played well would become a high-performing athlete over time.

The bet on young players ended up being a huge success. It was the most profitable investment made by the club during my entire administration and paid off in a very short amount of time. Boca multiplied its initial investment by ten and earned an income of $30 million. The emblematic case of this bet was undoubtedly that of Juan Román Riquelme.

I remember when I asked Bilardo to give Riquelme a chance as a starter. Always wise, Bilardo told me that he wasn't ready yet. That he needed to mature before being able to handle the pressure that came with wearing the jersey. That moment arrived a few months later, against Unión at La Bombonera. Still under eighteen years of age, Riquelme went on the pitch and scored his first goal for Boca.

In terms of soccer, 1996 was a forgettable year. The renewal of the team began after the departure of Navarro Montoya, Fabbri, and Mac Allister, who had led the demands for higher bonuses. New players arrived, such as Abbondanzieri, Cagna, Rambert, Toresani, Cedrés, Cáceres, Pompei, and Latorre.

Diego Maradona was the undisputed star of the team. However, he was far from providing the extraordinary performance we had all seen. At that time, he held the tough record of having missed five consecutive penalties, something inexplicable. On the other hand, he strongly rejected Bilardo's leadership as a coach. The relationship between them was enormously complex. Both their personalities, passionate and temperamental, seemed destined to inevitably clash. After much work and endless conversations with them, I achieved what seemed impossible: for them to work together.

I will never forget that first game with Maradona and Bilardo on Friday, March 8, 1996. While renovations were under way at La Bombonera, we had arranged for Boca to play as the home team at Vélez stadium in the neighborhood of Liniers, at the other side the city. We won 4–0. It was all joy. We felt like we were on cloud nine.

I pause at this point because it meant another lesson for me that I think is valid for any leader. I was euphoric after that victory. "Now, a new story begins," I told myself. But Bilardo brought me back to reality. He stopped me in the locker room and told me one of the most important phrases I have ever heard him say, "Calm down, Mauricio. A match is not a championship."

Many times we fall into the temptation of confusing the dimensions of the achievements we obtain along the way. We believe that we have already reached the goal, when in reality we are just starting to cover the first meters of the race. Making a mistake at this point can be fatal.

The joy of that game was short-lived and I had to deeply reflect on the situation I was going through as a leader. A sense of order had not yet been established in the team and Maradona was a constant source of tension. True to his style, Diego did not accept the rules and Carlos was not able to enforce them. The club was a pressure cooker and I felt like it was about to explode.

Suddenly everything seemed to be going wrong. In June, Vélez beat us in a strange match in which the referee Javier Castrilli sent off Maradona, Carrizo, and Mac Allister. Overwhelmed, I made the decision to participate that night in *Fútbol de Primera*, the most important soccer program, which broadcast the day's goals. Castrilli's performance had outraged me. I told the presenters, Marcelo Araujo and Enrique Macaya Márquez, that I saw a conspiracy against Boca and even went as far as proposing a ridiculous idea: that Boca's fans stop going to stadiums where we played as visitors. It was a known fact that the revenue of any club grew exponentially when playing against Boca. Immediately, I realized I had the obligation to apologize and admit my mistake. The fans' anger cannot be expressed by the club's president. Beyond the anger I had as a Boca fan, as a leader, I had to fulfill my institutional role.

The string of bad moments included a tour in China during the championship that left us out of the local tournament. Claudio Caniggia returned to the club from Europe a week later than stipulated. When it was time to reopen the stadium after the renovations, what was supposed to be a celebration ended up being tarnished by a historic defeat against Gimnasia y Esgrima La Plata, who beat us to a shameful 6–0.

The situation with Caniggia became unsustainable and his salary had become an unbearable cost for the club. The reinforcements we had called upon were not adapting to the demands of our club. The team was doing poorly and Bilardo could not lead it. His personality played against him and conflicts became increasingly intense and confrontational with everyone: journalists, leaders, and players.

I found myself faced with one of the toughest decisions of my tenure as president of Boca. The fans continued to show their dissatisfaction with the coach. Although my relationship with Bilardo was excellent and based on enormous respect, he decided that he could no longer continue. He had completed the first year of a two-year contract, and we mutually agreed to terminate it. Carlos had come in search of rematch and got a defeat. A new lesson: soccer is unforgiving.

8

Saying No

There are few things more important in a leader's job than being able to say no. Saying yes is always easier, more comfortable, and simpler. When you say yes, it is possible that many will follow. No, on the other hand, is often a lonely utterance.

There were many occasions when as a leader I said no. The list of examples is very long and diverse. Saying no, the refusal to do something that undermines what one is convinced of, always results in an ethical guide for the leader himself and also for those who accompany him.

I have said no a thousand times and I would do it again a thousand times more. In soccer, in politics, and my personal life. A leader's "no" is always associated with a sense of responsibility, with taking care of the common project. I put a lot at stake with every "no" I uttered. That's where true leadership is played out.

In Boca, saying no had to do mainly with economic issues, with taking care of the club's balance sheet and finances. Sometimes saying no is tremendously difficult, especially when one is left alone and those around you believe that you should say yes. That inner noise challenges the ego and can make the leader be perceived as stubborn or whimsical in their refusal. That's what happened to me in 1997, when I had to face enormous pressures to bring José Luis Chilavert, the charismatic Vélez Sarsfield goalkeeper, to Boca. At that time, Bilardo had already left and a new chapter had begun with Héctor Veira as coach. The situation became fragile again. That was another lost year in sports while our main rival, River Plate, continued to accumulate championships.

The need for a new goalkeeper was evident. Córdoba had not yet arrived, and Guzmán and Navarro Montoya had already been there. Abbondanzieri was not yet ready to occupy the position. The demand for Chilavert was incessant. At a time before the social media revolution, we must imagine or remember the role that television, newspapers, and radio played with messages repeated day in and out announcing Chilavert's imminent transfer to Boca. Sooner or later, the clamor reached the board of directors.

In the meeting room, the atmosphere was suffocating. Some spoke, shouted, and interrupted one another to demand the signing of Chilavert. Only a few of us were on the other side: the vice president, the treasurer, two or three members of the commission, and me. The price requested for the transfer was exorbitant: $5 million plus $1.5 million in salary per year, which tripled what the most expensive players in the squad received.

Once I managed to calm down the situation, I suggested listening to the arguments of each member of the committee. Everyone talked about Chilavert's charisma, how he was a very special player, about what he could mean for Boca, that he was the player we needed to start winning championships, and so on. Finally, it was my turn to speak.

As had been the case many times before, I knew I was defeated before saying anything. I decided to speak without making any personal speculation. I simply wanted to be true to my convictions and be heard. Emotional and sincere words came out of me.

I went straight to the point. I spoke of the pride I felt for presiding over the board of directors that had renovated the stadium, balanced the accounts, and modernized the club. I reminded them that the youth division, one of the best in the country, was up and running. I also acknowledged that I was fully aware that as far as soccer performance went, we had not given the fans the joy they demanded. But at one point, I decided to be categorical and stated that under no circumstances was I willing to financially sink Boca Juniors. I asked them to reflect for a moment on one of the great truths of soccer and any field: "No player by themselves guarantees the success of the team." At that moment, I launched a phrase that still resonates in my memory: "Maybe my destiny is to be a non-winning president. But I'm not going to bankrupt Boca to sign a player."

Perhaps that day was the first time I faced a recurring problem in the Argentine leadership culture. The idea of finding the shortcut, the magic solution that changes everything overnight, or the arrival of the providential man. They are illusions. Mirages of soccer and politics. All those paths do in the medium term is make you go back to the starting point.

I thought I had managed to contain the anxiety of the board of directors with my message. But I was wrong and the calm did not last long. A few weeks later, Maradona called me. Diego wanted me to hear it directly from him that although he deeply detested Chilavert, he understood that the team needed him. He asked me to think about it again. Along with Maradona, the coaching staff also insisted on bringing in the Paraguayan goalkeeper. I felt trapped. I had no other option. I had to agree.

I too used to dream of Chilavert scoring a goal against River with a free kick. It was a tempting and wonderful image. But beyond my fantasies, I knew that the financial aspect would bring countless problems in the locker room. I met with the board of directors again and stated that I was willing to make a single offer for Chilavert. It would be $3 million and not a dollar more, including expenses. I managed to make both the board and Maradona understand that this was the highest possible price. Any higher amount, as Vélez intended, would have been an abuse. Should the operation go through, it would be a mortgage destined to weigh on the club's finances for several years. The board accepted my proposal but there was one last missing step: to meet with Raúl Gámez, president of the Vélez Sarsfield club and holder of the goalkeeper's transfer.

Gámez welcomed me kindly but with a hint of arrogance in a room at the Argentine Football Association (Asociación de Fútbol Argentino, AFA) on Viamonte Street. Of course, he was aware of the back and forth regarding Chilavert's transfer to Boca. He was sure that he would finally get what he had asked for. I asked him for some financing, and to my surprise, he said that we could pay half of it in cash and the other half in thirty days. Things were not going well. For my proposal to be financially sustainable, we needed at least a year to pay the operation's total amount.

When I told Gámez that Boca's offer was $3 million, he turned as red as a tomato. The smile was gone, he looked at me angrily and said that he was not going to accept anything below $5 million. I told him that the offer I had given him was my only and final offer.

Angry, the president of Vélez told me that he had nothing else to say to me. The offer had been rejected. For my part, I admit that I couldn't help but smile from ear to ear. Gámez was offended. He thought I was laughing at him. "What are you laughing at? What's so funny?" he said, fuming. I told him the truth. I was relieved. I didn't know how we would have paid him if he had accepted. I told him that I thought I was crazy for offering such a huge amount of money for a goalkeeper who was thirty-five years old and already approaching the end of his career, but that I had discovered that there was someone even crazier than me. Someone who was capable of rejecting such an offer. He replied with an unforgettable phrase, "Forget it! Without Chilavert, you will never become a champion."

Of course, Gámez was wrong. But the problem remained. Boca still needed a goalkeeper. A few days later, the signing of Óscar Córdoba was another moment when intuition and reason played as allies in the decision-making process. It happened after the arrival of another player, Patrón Bermúdez, and just before completing that extraordinary trio of Colombians that gave so much to Boca with the arrival of Mauricio "Chicho" Serna.

When it came to Córdoba's transfer, we had agreed with his representative on $600,000. The meeting took place forty-eight hours later, on a Saturday in my office at the club. Óscar, a very serious and formal person, was, as always, immaculately dressed, while I arrived in shorts after playing a game of tennis. I didn't know which one of us was more out of place in that scene, him or me.

Once we were seated and with the papers ready to be signed, Carlos Quieto, the Colombian goalkeeper's representative, told me that there was a problem. That they had thought it over and believed that Córdoba's value was now $1.5 million. The representative's sentence left me speechless.

Quieto's argument was that he knew Boca had been in talks for Chilavert and, what was even worse, they were aware of the extraordinary amount of money that had been thrown around, those $5 million. Offended, Córdoba and his manager believed that if the Paraguayan national team goalkeeper was worth $5 million, the Colombian national team goalkeeper couldn't have a price lower than $1.5 million.

I couldn't believe my ears. Faced with such a change in conditions, I stood up impolitely and announced that the operation was cancelled. "You have no word," I told Córdoba and Quieto, who looked surprised. Now I was the angry one, and without saying anything else, I left the office, went to the parking lot, got into my car, started the engine, and as I was leaving through the Del Valle Ibarlucea exit, my cell phone rang.

It was Iván Pavlovsky, then head of Boca's press office. Iván was calling me to tell me that he had received information that in that precise moment, Maradona and Chilavert were on their way to Gámez's house. Together, they were determined to convince the president of Vélez to accept the proposal that he had turned down and thus allow his goalkeeper to move to Boca.

I realized that in the face of this new risk, my only option was Córdoba, practically an unknown player in Argentina. And to top it all off, the deal had just fallen through.

Once I hung up the phone, I left the car badly parked in front of the club and ran back to my office. Córdoba and Quieto were exiting the elevator. They were surprised to see me come back and I said to them, "Let's start over." It hadn't been more than five minutes since my abrupt departure from the meeting. They looked perplexed and agreed to return to the office to continue the conversation.

That was an extremely tough negotiation. After much discussion, we were stuck with a difference of $200,000. They had reduced their demands to $1.2 million and I did not budge from my new offer of $1 million. Quieto told me he couldn't lower the price anymore and suggested that I speak on the phone with his boss to try to convince him. I asked who his boss was and he replied that it was a man named Gilberto, who was in jail, but could speak from there. In an instant, I realized that it was probably a drug trafficker. Negotiating with soccer agents is something I have done many times. However, negotiating with a drug lord is something I have never done and always preferred to avoid, so I politely declined his invitation to talk and agreed to pay the $1.2 million and consider the matter resolved. Sometime later, I found out that the "boss" who was detained and to whom Quieto reported to was none other than Gilberto Rodríguez Orejuela, one of Colombia's most notorious drug traffickers, a shareholder of the America club and founder of the Cali Cartel.

I ended up paying considerably more than what we had agreed two days before for Córdoba's transfer. It could be considered a mistake but I don't think it was. The alternative was the $5 million for Chilavert, with a much higher salary than that of the team's main stars. Once they found out, the situation would soon have become explosive and complaints would have ensued.

As a strange paradox, I overpaid for Córdoba to prevent Boca from going bankrupt. It was a good decision in the medium term with a higher cost in the short term. All thanks to a timely phone call and to having learned to say no.

Once the deal was closed, we communicated it immediately. Boca had a new goalkeeper. Needless to say, Córdoba was one of the pillars of the team we built. Later on, Óscar asked me what had made me go back that morning. Of course, I told him the truth. I had made a hotheaded decision. I was certain that having Córdoba was the best possible way out of the dilemma I was facing. What had been right, that is, abandoning the negotiation after an unexpected change in conditions, could've led the way to an error that would've damaged the club's financial health. Boca came first, above all else, even above the popular solution—or perhaps I should write "populist"—that focused on hiring Chilavert.

A few months later, another difficult "no" would come. After losing a tournament by one point, Bambino started the next championship poorly. Despite his best efforts and that famous phrase of "the foundation is there," Veira decided to resign. Shortly thereafter, the press began to spread the news that Diego Maradona wanted to be the new Boca coach. The idea began to grow with unusual strength. Overnight, the Boca universe was revolutionized. Diego had all the qualifications for the position. He was linked to the club like no other player, and the Xeneize fans had built with him a relationship of absolute and unconditional idolatry.

Diego had been struggling with serious personal difficulties related to drug use for some time. The media and the world of soccer had raised a huge wall of silence regarding the issue. No one wanted to publicly talk about Maradona's addictions. Meanwhile, at Boca, the board of directors wanted to move forward with the hiring, which made me face a new dilemma. I had no choice and decided to deal with it.

Luis Conde organized the meeting with Diego at his house. An impeccable-looking Maradona arrived about ten minutes after the agreed meeting time. At first, he gave me the impression of being healthy. As soon as he saw me, he smiled with that mischievous and unforgettable smile and asked me, "Are you willing to go down in history as the most important soccer executive in the world?"

I felt a jolt to my ego. I remained silent for a few moments, enough to realize that what he was proposing was real. I knew that hiring Maradona in the condition he was in was a decision that carried a very high risk. As the seconds ticked by, I said to myself, *Remember, you're not here for your ego. You're here for Boca, for the institution. Don't forget that.*

I didn't answer. I smiled uncomfortably at such a challenge and we sat down in the living room. We were face-to-face. My idol and the greatest glory of Argentine soccer with all his charisma, and me, the president of Boca who had lost his coach.

"Diego, no one more than you deserves to sit on the bench to manage Boca. No one represents Boca and no one has the unconditional love of the fans like you do, that's crystal clear to me. But there is an issue," I began.

Diego, like many addicts, was deeply irritated when his health was discussed. It was a forbidden topic. It was understandable. The world of soccer had made him believe he was a god or a demigod. But Maradona was like any other human being. Along with his incomparable talent as a soccer player, he also had, like everyone, weaknesses and flaws. I decided to use a euphemism. "First, we should fix the little problem," I said, trying to address the issue that worried me the most.

Diego took some time and started muttering, "Little problem, little problem, little problem…" He spent a few seconds seemingly thinking about his response, and then he said, "Well, let's assume that I have a little problem… We call a press conference, you announce that I am the new coach of Boca, and I say that I'm going to start a treatment to solve the little problem. What do you think?"

Conde was enthusiastic and said that he thought that Diego's proposal was excellent. A treatment would take months, and in the meantime, he could work as the coach. He looked at me then, as if seeking my approval. But no, it was not possible to accept the proposal. It is a well-known fact that addiction treatments are incredibly complex. Despite everything, I insisted on my position, "No, Diego, not like that. First you have to solve the problem. And then, you have my word of honor that the position of head coach will be yours."

In my mind, there was room for hope. The idea of seeing Maradona coaching Boca filled me with enthusiasm and hope, like any fan. But there was something that sounded like an alarm. The experiment could go wrong, and the responsibility would fall on me. We couldn't count on Diego when we didn't know where and how he would be the next day. I knew that his recovery was a nonnegotiable condition to build that new career that made us all so hopeful and which would undoubtedly bring glory to the club.

Diego, as quick as ever, replied that he first wanted to be the coach of Boca and then he would have no problem dealing with the solution to his "little problem." I said no and went back to square one. First, the "little problem," then Boca. Boca was the most important thing.

After listening to me, there was a silence that seemed to go on forever. I don't know how long it lasted, maybe a minute or more. His body and face became extremely tense, his eyes looked as if they were about to pop out of their sockets. It was the same enraged look he had after the fourth goal against Greece in the US World Cup. Diego's smile began to transform in slow motion into an expression of visceral hatred that I had never seen before, nor would I see again.

Suddenly, he jumped out of his seat and shouted at me, "You will regret this moment for the rest of your life!" I tried to continue the conversation without raising my voice, but I was not successful. "You know what, Mauricio? I will destroy you! I will crush you to pieces! Mark my words, I will destroy you!"

The meeting ended at that precise moment. I remained silent. I felt like there was nothing left to say. At the same time, I began to feel an enormous sadness. That man, capable of so many feats, who had won everything, was telling me in his own way that the only thing he couldn't do was overcome himself.

That was how Maradona didn't become the coach of Boca. And that is also how my personal relationship with Diego ended. We spoke again years later, when I called him in Cuba, where he was undergoing treatment, to offer him the Boca stadium for his farewell match. I was aware that beyond any differences, there was no better place for Diego to say goodbye to soccer. I remember he was surprised, and we had a warm conversation. On November 10, 2001, we met again at La Bombonera. It was when he uttered that memorable phrase: *"La pelota no se mancha"* (the ball should not be stained) meaning the untouchable beauty of soccer was above personal circumstances. That afternoon, I gave him a plaque on behalf of the club. We hadn't seen each other since that meeting at Conde's house. In that packed stadium, he looked at me and said, "You?" I could only reply, "Yes, me."

Over time, his disputes with me shifted to politics, and we found ourselves on opposite sides on countless occasions. However, my admiration for him as a soccer player remains intact from the first day I saw him play many years ago, when he was a rising star wearing the Argentinos Juniors jersey.

Not choosing Maradona was perhaps the toughest and most difficult decision I ever had to make. Time would prove me right. Without Diego, we were able to build a strong institution that put the blue and gold colors above all others. Institutions are always the most important thing. It was this, above all else, that made Boca a brilliant team capable of winning everything.

9

The Beginning of Change

Martín Palermo would have never played for Boca if I had not made a mistake before. In 1996, shortly after starting my tenure, I received a call from the famous agent Gustavo Mascardi. He told me about a Chilean forward that he thought was ideal for Boca. I had a good relationship with Mascardi and we had already done some deals together. The agent sent me some videos, and I called Bilardo to watch them together and evaluate how Marcelo Salas played. Bilardo immediately gave up, "Mauricio, we already have many forwards. We have Carrario, Rambert, Cedrés. Why buy one more?"

I stayed home alone watching the videos, sitting in front of the television. You didn't need to be a specialist to realize that I was in front of an exceptional player who possessed an extraordinary mix of skills and strength. Anyone who has watched as many soccer matches as I have can quickly distinguish exceptional players. Salas was one of them.

Mascardi kept insisting. "Look, he's one of those players that only appear once in a long while. You can't lose him," he said on the other side of the phone. I decided to talk to Bilardo again. Carlos, who is above all an austere man, reluctantly watched some videos and ended up accepting, somewhat reluctantly, "Alright, bring him. We'll do something with him."

With the coach's approval, I proposed the purchase of Salas to the board of directors. None of them agreed. The problem was Mascardi. "We already bought Cáceres and Verón from Mascardi. Enough!" some said. "This is not Mascardi's team!" shouted those on the other side of the table. While they argued, I thought to myself, *I better forget about Salas and move on.*

I did not move on. I kept thinking that Salas was destined to be one of the great soccer stars in our country, as he confirmed shortly after in River. In light of what happened later, I don't regret not having signed him. Without Salas, Boca won countless tournaments, both locally and internationally.

However, I find in this story a mistake that I try to avoid as much as possible: going against yourself. That time, I didn't listen to my own convictions and acted under the pressure of those around me. I didn't stick to my guns, as they say. What happened to me is a mistake that should be avoided. The risk is nothing less than losing oneself. One should never lose their identity. Julio Grondona, the eternal AFA president, was right when he told me, "The costs of not doing what one believes one should do will come, sooner or later."

Just as I lost Salas by not listening to my gut, I managed to add another great player, Martín Palermo, by doing the opposite. Once again, I had to sit down and negotiate with

Mascardi, who had told me about the possibility of making an offer. Palermo had the essential qualities to be a great player for Boca: an eccentric personality with a lot of self-confidence. He was someone who was capable of facing that enormous wave that one must surf to become a star at Boca. A player capable of not being crushed by the volatile passion of the fans. He had something special. A gift.

As had been the case with Salas and Bilardo, I went to talk to Bambino Veira, who was the coach at the time, and I came out somewhat disappointed. He told me that he felt Martín would not have a place on the team, as we already had Caniggia, Latorre, Cedrés, and Rambert. I insisted and he finally accepted. He promised me that he would test him in the next Mercosur Cup.

With Salas, I had learned my lesson. This time, I was going all in. I met with the board of directors and told them that I was convinced that we should buy Palermo. I said confidently, "Palermo is the new Tanque Rojas." Some panicked, but most believed me. Luck was also on our side, as at that very moment River decided to buy Rambert. With that money, we had the necessary sum for the purchase of Palermo and Guillermo Barros Schelotto. A few days later, Palermo made his debut in the Mercosur Cup.

If there was a moment that marked the beginning of Boca's golden era, it was on September 3, 1997. I will never forget it. That day, the most successful forward line in Boca's history was born and the club began its great record in the history of Argentine soccer.

In the case of Palermo, I placed my convictions above myself. I avenged my lack of determination when it came to the possibility of Salas. I had lost and won. From then on, another chapter began for Boca and for me. I went through the crisis that was summarized in Diego Latorre's phrase when he said that "Boca is a cabaret" due to the disputes that were taking place in the locker room. The team continued to add great players like Vasco Arruabarrena and others and, despite losing the championship that year by one point, I began to experience a certainty that I had not felt until then: the change had finally begun.

Veira's departure drove me to having to make one of the most important decisions as president: I had to choose the new coach. It was never an easy task.

I had in front of me a list of great coaches made up of Daniel Passarella, Miguel Brindisi, and Carlos Bianchi. All three expressed different values and concepts. All three had completely different personalities. Which one would be the best for Boca?

The team that Bianchi led in Vélez had something that had awakened my admiration as a soccer lover. It's difficult to put it into words. A confidence, a camaraderie, a special way of giving oneself. In that Vélez, there was a sense of team. A common sports project among all the players aligned with the coaching staff. I must admit that the playing style proposed by Bianchi did not arouse great passions in me. I saw it as somewhat conservative for my taste. But I saw in that team something akin to a positive atmosphere, a method, a security, and a solidarity coming from the bench. The best word to define it is, precisely, leadership. I concluded that Bianchi was the person that Boca needed. The choice of previous coaches had been made with the consensus of other directors. This time, I had a certainty, and I decided to risk all my credibility on it.

I was determined to persuade the "Virrey" to come back to Argentina and coach Boca. The unforgettable Eduardo Gamarnik, a huge Boca fan and one of my most important advisers during my tenure, organized the meeting. It took place in a hotel in Spain. We didn't know each other personally. Throughout the conversation, I felt like time had stopped. Before I knew it, we had been talking about soccer for more than six hours. I discovered that he wasn't an easy person, despite his enormous confidence and self-assurance. He was hurting because things hadn't gone well for him in Roma and expressed his desire to return to coaching in our country.

Thanks to the wise advice of Bilardo and Veira, Boca had already put together a great squad. The process had taken less time than Bilardo had predicted, but now we needed a coach who had the ability to give coherence to that group of people.

Bianchi confirmed my best feelings. His method was key to showcase what I had been obsessed with since before arriving at Boca. To achieve the proposed objectives, one must be coherent, work within an order, be persistent, and remain true to oneself.

Bianchi allowed me to make my biggest bet, the one I needed the most. To show (and prove to myself) that I wasn't just the club's president who would fix the stadium and run it efficiently. That my own prophecy about being a "non-winning president" wouldn't come true. Around the soccer world, there was the idea that I didn't know anything about soccer, that I thought Boca was a business, that I had no idea what it took to win a championship. At times, I myself began to doubt and wonder if there was some truth to that.

I embraced the idea of bringing Bianchi as one embraces a cause. His arrival represented the possibility of demonstrating that we were capable of being competitive if our organization had the leadership it needed. But not everyone was on board. Once again, I was in the minority.

The majority of the board of directors supported the arrival of Passarella as coach. The fans were divided. Some supported the idea and, above all, felt that bringing Passarella to Boca was like stealing a symbol from River. To others, it was outrageous to summon someone so closely associated with our eternal rival. The tension grew as my conviction to tempt Bianchi remained strong.

Like the classic movie *Twelve Angry Men*, where one member of a jury convinces the other eleven to change their vote, I felt like I had an impossible task ahead of me. Pedro Pompilio had already told me that he supported my idea, but we would have to convince the others of the advantages of having Bianchi. One by one, we did it. It was an incredible act of persuasion. It took us some time, but little by little we turned them around and managed to get the support of the majority.

In July 1998 Carlos Bianchi arrived in Argentina. He was Boca Juniors' new coach.

10

We Are the Champions

There comes a day, a specific moment, when you realize that things are finally changing. That the ground is shifting. Having the opportunity to lead a transformation is an incomparable privilege. Feeling that your work is beginning to bear fruit is unique. It is confirmation that all the effort, all the frustrations, the accumulated anger, and the bad times served a purpose. The *what for* is no longer a promise; it becomes a tangible reality.

With Bianchi everything changed. In the goal, Óscar Córdoba started to become the Córdoba that Boca fans remember, thanks to the confidence that the coach placed in him on his first day. Walter Samuel began to continuously improve. Hugo Ibarra proved that adding him to the team was totally hit the mark. Patrón Bermúdez lived up to his nickname and owned the defense. Vasco Arruabarrena was capable of defending and attacking at the same time. Chicho Serna recovered all the balls and earned the unconditional love of those in the stands. Diego Cagna, Pepe Basualdo, Juan Román Riquelme, Martín Palermo, and Guillermo Barros Schelotto played soccer by heart, as if they had known one another since childhood.

That team was everything. And it showed everything. It filled stadiums all over the world, won two championships undefeated. It remained unbeaten for forty games and broke all records. Boca was a giant that had awakened. Everyone began to realize it.

That team transformed me and all the Boca fans. Together we left behind years of failures. We shouted, got emotional, jumped, and celebrated like never before. The time of mistakes, inexperience, illusions, and disappointments had been left behind. One game summarizes all those emotions. It was the classic match against River at La Bombonera in the Copa Libertadores de América quarterfinals. That was much more than a simple soccer match.

It was a Wednesday night, more precisely, May 24, 2000. I remember it as if it had happened yesterday. we had just pitifully tied a game in the local championship despite dominating for ninety minutes. Then we went to Núñez to play the first leg of the Copa's quarterfinals as visitors and lost 2–1. Ahead of us was a week of anxiety and gritted teeth. The whole country was talking about it. Boca had to turn around a very difficult result.

Much has been written about the beauty of soccer. There are occasions when a team manages to achieve collective feats that seem to go beyond reality. Marcelo Delgado opened the scoring in the fourteenth minute of the second half: 1–0. A silence full of tension seemed to fall upon the players on the pitch. With that result, we were out of the cup.

Fifty thousand people in the stadium and millions at home held their breath. Time stood still. Yet the clock continued to inexorably advance. At seventy-seven minutes, Bianchi brought in Palermo for Alfredo Moreno. Martín had been out for six months with a knee ligament injury. La Bombonera seemed to come alive. It shook and a roar greeted the entry of the striker.

As if a supernatural force had come from somewhere, at the eighty-fourth minute, after a penalty was awarded for a foul against Battaglia, Riquelme scored the second goal and we all breathed again. Until the ninetieth minute. Palermo received the ball near the penalty spot and began to position himself in slow motion. He seemed to move his body without any hurry, in control of himself and the clock. The seconds passed slowly, seemingly lasting for hours. Palermo looked forward and kicked with his left foot. The ball went in: 3–0. The end.

That night Boca made history. And I was there, like the kid who dreamed of scoring the championship goal, being part of that same history. I never lived a game like that again. I doubt it will ever happen again. I was euphoric. I put aside any protocol as I celebrated with whoever crossed my path toward the locker room.

Some consider me a cold person. Nothing could be further from the truth. That night, Martin and I hugged under the shower, he was naked and I was dressed. All of my personal history with Boca was concentrated in that moment. It was very intense. That celebration, that infinite stream of joy, was the way to express the success that comes after a long wait, a lot of work, a lot of suffering. A great satisfaction that goes beyond having eliminated none other than River to reach the semifinals of a tournament. It was something else. It was Boca, that unique passion, at times childish, at times painful, but always incomparable.

Everything that came afterward was very difficult. We managed to reach the final in Mexico, at Estadio Azteca, against America in a heart-stopping match. The final was against Palmeiras from Brazil. In the first match at La Bombonera, we played poorly and barely managed a 2–2 draw thanks to Arruabarrena's talent. We had to play the second leg at Morumbi stadium in São Paulo. It is a pitch where the pressure of the home crowd is felt in a different way. The weight of the local fans at Morumbi is a phenomenon similar to what happens at La Bombonera.

The morning after the first final, I decided to call Bianchi. I asked to see him at home before he went to training. I had spent the previous night thinking about the game we had ahead of us and felt an urgent need to talk to him.

It was very cold on that June morning. Bianchi arrived somewhat annoyed. He hadn't even had a chance to take off his overcoat when he said, "I know, Mauricio, you're going to tell me the same thing that all the fans have been telling me since last night. That we played horribly, that we were a disaster, and that we lost the cup."

However, my goal in summoning Carlos that morning was very different. "Indeed, we were a disaster. But you know what? I'm sure we're going to win this cup. That's why I called you. If we go out there and park the bus, they'll kill us. We have to play them on equal footing. I'm sure that's how we'll beat them," I replied.

Bianchi looked at me first with suspicion, and then his expression began to change. He jumped up and started to smile: "I agree. Our chance is intact. We are going to win this cup!" he said, confident in himself.

Backing others up is a leader's undivided responsibility. A leader who withholds support from those who accompany him is not up to the demands of that position. When things do not go as planned, when it seems that objectives will not be achieved, when discouragement wants to make one give up, that's where the value and mystery of leadership must kick in.

After a week of hard work by the coaching staff with the squad, what had to happen happened. Córdoba became a true giant with those unforgettable penalties in the shootout. I cried like a child. Boca had once again won an international title. There I was, at forty-one, fulfilling my *what for*. Confirming the choice I had made five years earlier to change the course of my life to devote myself to fulfilling a dream for myself and for so many Boca fans who accompanied me. I was happy. Crazy with joy. And just when it seemed like everything was returning to normal, the trip to Japan came. There we went, heading to the match against Real Madrid at the National Stadium in Tokyo, for the Intercontinental Cup.

Soccer players have very particular codes. The internal climate, the atmosphere that is experienced inside a team, is inaccessible from the outside. It is not easy for a manager, a fan, or a journalist to know the reality of what happens in the locker rooms. It is a different world and it's practically impossible to know for sure how the different moments, tensions, conflicts, and rivalries among the different groups that make up a high-performance sports team are experienced.

At Boca, I had the help of a person who was of enormous importance when it came to translating the secret language of the players. Alfredo "el Tanque" Rojas fulfilled this function perfectly. A soccer player's DNA ran in Rojas's blood. He had shone like few others in the Boca of my childhood, he had built himself up from a very humble origin, had played in Europe, and had returned to Argentina at a time when soccer was not yet hyper-professionalized. Rojas understood the mind of the Boca player like no other.

Before boarding the plane to play the final in Japan, el Tanque told me he wanted to talk to me. "Mauricio, I'm very worried. There's a fracture in the team. There are some guys who are fighting and you can't play good soccer like that," he said. I imagined what was happening and Rojas confirmed it to me. The problem was that, on one hand, Palermo wanted Guillermo Barros Schelotto by his side on the pitch. On the other, Riquelme was pressuring the coach to have his friend Delgado in that position. Riquelme had a point in his favor. Delgado was playing very well. He was very confident and had acquired great speed.

By then, Bianchi had distanced himself from the discussions and internal differences among the players. Taking the pulse of what happens within the team is another inescapable responsibility of any leader. How each one is doing, what they need, what conflicts may exist with their teammates. It's not about being one of the boys in the group because the roles are different. I have already written about the dangers that come with the isolation of a leader.

We had just arrived in Tokyo and I decided to talk to Carlos for a minute in the locker room while the players were doing their first training session. "Carlos, you have to break this tension between Martín and Román. The cost can be very serious. A conflict like this is going to prevent the magic from happening, be careful." Bianchi didn't let me finish and replied that no, absolutely not, that I was wrong, that the team was solid. I left the locker room worried, thinking that it's never good to deny problems.

Something happened later, as I found out afterward. At the end of the training session, Carlos locked himself in the dressing room with all the players. There was a great catharsis. They said everything they had to say to each other and the tension disappeared. The bond had been restored. The group regained its *what for*.

I don't know if my warning influenced Bianchi's attitude. But it was clear that Carlos had changed his mind and exercised his own leadership over the group. He finally made a clear decision: Delgado was a starter and was on the pitch alongside Martín Palermo.

I experienced it as if it were a dream. At times, I had to convince myself that what was happening before my eyes was true. Palermo's two goals came and the Real Madrid's goal followed. Millions of clenched teeth were waiting for the referee's final whistle, which seemed to never come.

I had fulfilled my promise. Boca was where I had dreamed it should be: on top of the world. Seven thousand Boca fans had gathered in Japan. It was something never seen before. They came from different parts of the world, from Europe, Asia, America, Africa, and Oceania to watch their team.

Far from blowing over, that victory grew in magnitude over the years. It was Boca's greatest moment of glory. After that match, Real Madrid never lost a final again. Florentino Pérez, the legendary Madridista president with whom I maintain a great friendship, still reminds me of it today. "I will never be able to forget that final you won against us in Japan," he says every time we meet. That great "Galácticos" team made the biggest mistake that no one ever and under no circumstances should make: underestimate the opponent.

The return to Argentina was incredible. People poured out onto the streets en masse to see the bus carrying the world champions pass by. As I looked out the window at the joyful faces along the route from the airport, I began to ponder the meaning of everything I had done and built over those five years. There had been years of loneliness. Saying no to Maradona, my greatest sporting hero, had been the right decision. I found myself thinking about the strength of perseverance, the importance of maintaining coherence despite all obstacles, and the peace of mind that comes from having a great team.

I was able to understand that my *what for* was no longer exclusive. It was a collective *what for*, built with the contribution that everyone had made from the institution to reach the moment of triumph. I wanted to thank each one of them, from the first to the last person, because we had gotten there thanks to everyone sharing the same objectives, with the same *what for*. From the players and the coaching staff to the countless men and women who had put in time, work, conviction, and enthusiasm.

On that bus, surrounded by Boca players, is when I came to a definitive conclusion: No matter what they say, if you work hard enough, dreams can come true.

11

Enough is Enough

Life is made up of cycles. Knowing how to read and interpret them is an art. When does a new cycle begin? When does it end? In mid-2001, the time had come to talk to Carlos Bianchi about his continuity as coach of Boca Juniors. Changes in cycles, viewed from a leadership perspective, are extremely delicate moments.

We sat down to talk in a hotel. I came to the meeting imagining that I would have a tough economic negotiation ahead of me. With Boca Juniors, Bianchi had become one of the most prestigious coaches in the world and his success was beyond discussion. I had heard that a group of Barcelona officials, with all their sporting and economic power behind them, were lurking, sounding out the coach to see if he was willing to continue his career with them in Spain.

Carlos's first sentence left me speechless. "Look, Mauricio, we've won too many things together. Sometimes you have to know when to call it a day." He then confessed his desire to go to Barcelona. It wasn't good news, as there were still six months left to fulfill the contract with Boca.

Despite the utter shock, I tried to show understanding. I told him that I wouldn't put any obstacles in his way if going to Spain was his objective and I expressed my enormous gratitude for everything he had done for Boca during his time with us.

While we were in the meeting, an idea came to me that could bring us closer together. I wanted to know if he would be willing to make a commitment. Since nothing had been signed yet, I proposed that, if the Barcelona deal fell through, he consider continuing his work for two more years at Boca.

From the beginning, Bianchi had an incentive in his contract to bet on young players and the club's academy. When a player was sold, Carlos received a percentage of the operation based on the increase in the value of the transfer after having passed through Boca. It was a great idea that led him to bet on young players on numerous occasions.

At that moment, the team was going through a complex situation. A group of players was leaving the club while some replacements would soon join them. I wanted the new team to be able to benefit from Bianchi's imprint. I was convinced that Carlos's presence was key to keeping the team from falling apart and maintaining the winning spirit that had characterized him.

The deal with Barcelona fell through and 2001 was a mediocre year in terms of results. We were knocked out of the Mercosur Cup and we started the local championship on the wrong foot. In soccer, the usual thing is for winning to be just an interval in between defeats. As usual in these cases, and despite Bianchi's glorious record at Boca, some small sectors began to make themselves heard with criticisms against the coach.

By then, I had already learned to put this type of reactions into perspective. Every time a few matches pass without the team winning, fans become increasingly nervous. The joys of the previous year are forgotten, they become the past. Criticisms coming from outside can be a disruptive element for leadership. Soccer taught me not to let myself be affected by the enormous tangle of comments that surround it. This does not mean not listening. On the contrary, the idea is to avoid the noise, the murmur, the rumors. However, despite not paying too much attention to the matter, I realized that it was affecting Carlos. A lot. At first, it was just a certain annoyance, but after a while, his irritation was impossible to hide.

A few weeks later, Carlos brought up the topic one more time. Once again, he wanted to tell me that he felt his cycle at Boca had to come to an end when his contract expired. He sounded more convinced. I asked him to give me some time and decided to play one last card. I asked Goyo Zidar, who was in charge of amateur soccer at the club, to try to open a new negotiation with Carlos. They started to talk, had some meetings, and things seemed to be heading toward a happy conclusion.

I don't remember when or why, but during those days in September, I was taking a course on Borges that was being taught at the Ministry of Foreign Affairs. As I listened to the discussion of the different themes that run through the works of the author of *Fictions*, I felt my phone vibrate in my pocket. I looked at the screen and saw a missed call and a voicemail from Carlos. I waited a while until there was a break and left the classroom to listen to it.

Bianchi's voice spoke to me from the phone and said, "Hi, Mauricio, I want you to know that I have given it a lot of thought. Last night I talked with my family. I am now heading to a press conference that I called to announce my decision not to continue in the club. Oh… I have already told the players."

I felt a deep sorrow. His message was the kind that didn't leave any room for a response. In other words, he was telling me that we had nothing left to discuss. It was a done deal.

I felt that I had no choice but to consider three and a half years of respect, shared work, achievements, and care as concluded. For Carlos, there seemed to be no turning back. In a state of shock from the news, I looked for a private place and called him. The night before, we had spoken for more than an hour, and he had not hinted at the decision that he had evidently already taken.

His response was abrupt. "That's it, Mauricio. It's not worth it for us to keep talking. It's best for both of us to end it. It's not the end of the world for anyone, much less for Boca."

He left me with no options. I told him I agreed that Boca was more important than him and even myself. Nobody is indispensable. Boca had a century of history and had existed before we even came into this world and will continue to exist long after we have departed. Nevertheless, I insisted. I pointed out that it didn't make any sense to announce that he was abandoning ship when he still had six months left on his contract. Carlos then gave me a new reason that explained his desire to leave. "Mauricio, I believe that soon you're going to go into politics and you're going to leave Boca. I came with you, and I want to leave with you."

The year 2001 was terrible, one of the worst years in our entire history. The convertibility plan was approaching its end, and with it, Argentina was facing the return of political and economic instability. The catastrophe seemed inevitable, and President Fernando de la Rúa's government was trying to postpone the outcome as long as possible. In that turbulent context, I had committed myself to the Creer y Crecer Foundation alongside Francisco de Narváez. The idea of doing something for Argentina had started to take shape in my mind, but I had no doubts in assuring Carlos that whatever role I played in politics, he had my word that I would be in the club until the last day of my term. We concluded the conversation.

That solid and self-assured Carlos Bianchi that I had met in Spain had become a man who was increasingly hard and uncompromising. A rough and complex component had been taking up more and more space in his personality. For my part, I tried to imagine what was going on inside his head. When you win one, two, three, four, five, six championships, others offer you an enlarged image of yourself. An exaggeration that makes you believe that you are some sort of Superman, someone with the ability to turn everything you touch into a success. But when you lose the seventh or eighth tournament, everything changes overnight. This abrupt change is a breeding ground for depression. In that situation, it's easy to feel useless and incapable of recovering the glory.

Carlos felt that the 1998 team with which we had won everything had been irretrievably lost. We had reached the pinnacle and the following day appeared uncertain in the eyes of the coach. It was not difficult for me to understand his situation. I myself had gone through that period when I imagined going down in Boca's history as a "non-winning president." At the same time, I had learned that success is always circumstantial and never eternal.

A few days after that phone conversation, I read a headline in a newspaper that filled me with confusion: "Bianchi leaves Boca because the directors don't want him despite his willingness to stay." If there was one thing I was sure of, was that things hadn't been like that. The entire board of directors wanted Carlos to continue. The next day, I called him again and left a message that went unanswered. "Carlos, I don't understand. No one in Boca wants you to leave. Please clarify what's going on because I need to know. It's one thing if you want to leave because you feel your cycle is over, but quite another if you feel like you are being let go. If there's a problem with the board of directors or within the team, please tell me so I can resolve it."

Knowing that our coach was going to leave months before it happened generated a huge uncertainty across the team. It's something I learned in the companies I worked for and later applied in politics. When someone decides to leave the team, the time that elapses between the decision and its implementation is usually very problematic.

Carlos's announcement at that time could jeopardize all the work done.

The Sunday after our conversation, we played against Lanús in La Bombonera. It was a great victory, 5–1. However, from the stands, there was a constant chant, "He's not leaving / Bianchi is not leaving," while insults rained down against the members of the board of directors suspected of objecting to the coach's continuity.

And it was then when I made a big mistake, which was also a great learning experience. Like so many times before, after the match I attended the press conference. There we had a failed conversation that the Argentine soccer world would never forget.

I entered the press conference and told Bianchi with total sincerity, "Carlos, in 1998 it was difficult to bring you in and establish you at the club because the fans had their hopes set on other candidates. However, today we all want you to stay. So, here and publicly, I ask you to tell me what the obstacles are and I promise to solve them as I have done during these three and a half years."

Carlos looked at me surprised, put his head in his hands and said nothing. I insisted, "I'm asking you to give me an answer. If you want to throw in the towel now because we have to work harder for what's coming in the future…" Things were getting worse by the minute. I kept waiting for a response from him. "Carlos, you have to give us an answer, because Boca fans deserve to know about the situation and for there to be no misunderstandings that lead to something as painful as what we're experiencing today, when Boca is a model institution. Just as we explained to everybody when we came here together for the first time what our project and commitment were, for the same reason we have to explain why the project is not continuing. I also need to know what the reasons are for the project not continuing!"

Serious and annoyed, Carlos replied that he wasn't going to talk about his contract and reiterated that he wouldn't continue at Boca beyond the end of the year limit. "I don't have to mention the reasons… let's not turn this into an afternoon talk show," he concluded firmly.

I insisted for the third time and demanded that he clarify that he had no problem with the board of directors. "It's not fair to the people of Boca that I am in the dark about what the problem is. If there's anything Boca can do to make you stay, Boca will do it. I want you to tell me that Boca cannot do anything and that you want to conclude this chapter. Tell me because what the press is saying isn't true," I said emphatically. And Carlos, in a gesture that would go down in history, got up as a sign of frustration and left in a huff.

The whole country talked about that press conference. Some even accused me of acting like a "ranch owner," giving free rein to all the prejudices that had been piling up since my arrival at Boca. Others told me that Carlos's attitude had been disrespectful, not toward me but toward the position I held as club president and that I should immediately terminate his contract and fire him, but once again I prioritized what was best for Boca.

Two days later, I met Carlos again for a meal in Puerto Madero and we settled our differences. I asked him to fulfill his contract until its end in December and to lead the team in the final of the Intercontinental Cup against Bayern Munich. I needed his authority on the sidelines and didn't want to risk the result of that important match. And I insisted once again but Bianchi replied that he had not been looked after well enough and that his reasons were strictly personal. He ended his response with the same phrase he used on the first day: "You have to know when to call it a day." For my part, at a new press conference, I apologized to those who felt offended by my attitude. I celebrated being able to dialogue and clarify things. "We had a difficult weekend for Boca. Sunday was sad and strange for me because we beat Lanús and I felt that the executives were taking the heat. Instead of enjoying the win, there were insults. For me, it was a mixture of anguish, pain, and anger. Without a doubt, my entrance was impulsive, maybe surprising. But it was driven by passion. That's why I want to apologize for the manners used on Sunday and ask the fans, coaching staff, executives, and players to stay united until the end of the year to confirm to the world that Boca is one of the greats of the soccer world."

After Bianchi's departure, the first of the two that he would experience, I hired Uruguayan Óscar Tabárez, who had already led Boca a decade ago. The Maestro, as he was known after years of teaching in schools in his country, held the coaching position throughout 2002. He did a great job, but a draw with Independiente at the end of the tournament left the rival at the doorstep of the title. By then, Bianchi had already expressed his desire to return to

Boca. Once again, and in spite of the ending we had had to his previous tenure, I told the members of the board of directors that I would never be an obstacle and that Boca would always come first. Those who believed that I would oppose something positive for the club out of personal reasons were once again mistaken. Thus, Bianchi returned to the club in 2003. By then, Riquelme had already been transferred to Barcelona.

The coexistence with Riquelme, a player who was often challenging and reluctant to accept any kind of limits, was a complex problem for Bianchi. I witnessed several instances of the player's disdainful behavior toward the coach during trainings and trips. On the eve of the final match against Bayern Munich in Tokyo, I remember sneaking into the practice to indulge in my childhood habit of kicking the ball around. All the players were running around the pitch, except for Riquelme, who instead made a half-hearted effort and lazily walked around the center line. He then approached the area where the coach stood alongside physical trainer Julio Santella, and I overheard him say, "Carlos, that's enough. I don't want to keep running around the pitch." Bianchi made a gesture of annoyance, and I pretended not to have heard and continued kicking the ball toward the goal. For Carlos, who had always been known for being very strict in terms of discipline and equal effort, a player wanting to impose their own training guidelines was unacceptable.

Riquelme's challenges to the coach's authority began to become more frequent over time. Sometimes they manifested in important issues, and at other times in minor details that generated enormous irritation in Carlos. In hindsight, I believe that these kinds of attitudes on the part of Riquelme were one of the factors that wore down Bianchi's authority over the team toward the end of his first stint.

The return of Bianchi to Boca was celebrated by the fans as a triumph. And the facts proved them right. Boca won the Copa Libertadores that year with a historic thrashing against the legendary Santos of Brazil, and we obtained the third Intercontinental Cup for the club against Milan in Japan.

Despite the successes, Bianchi's inner process led him to make some erratic soccer decisions. As I have written before, fans' patience is limited, and the coach's would turn out to be limited as well. After the defeat against Once Caldas of Colombia in the final of the Copa Libertadores, Bianchi withdrew the team from the pitch, refusing to receive the runners-up medals. It was an unsportsmanlike attitude that was also perceived as an institutional embarrassment by Boca, even though Bianchi later claimed it was a mistake due to ignorance of the protocol.

As we flew back from Colombia, we agreed to have a meeting at home to define the new team and the changes he was considering. He had barely crossed the threshold when Carlos announced to me, "I'm leaving."

"Are you leaving for a few days?" I responded, convinced that he was taking a vacation following the stress of the Libertadores final.

"No, Mauricio. I'm leaving the club. It's over. That's it. I came back, we won again. That's it."

The scene of two years ago was repeating itself. I wanted to be clear, so I said, "Carlos, it's a real shame what you're telling me, but let me ask you a question. Tomorrow, when I wake up and read the newspaper, am I going to read that Bianchi is leaving on his own accord or am I going to read again that he's leaving because the board of directors and the president of Boca don't want him anymore? Let's clarify it from the outset, shall we?" He assured me that he would always say that it was a personal decision and that Boca had nothing to do with it.

After the game, I sat down at my desk to listen to classical music. I wanted to know how long it would take for Iván Pavlovsky to call me. I knew that sooner or later, the journalists would get in touch with our press chief to ask him if it was true that Bianchi was leaving Boca. However, what interested me most was to learn what reasons were given. Until that moment, the only person at Boca who knew that Bianchi had resigned was me. A little while later, my phone rang. Of course, it was Pavlovsky: "Mauricio, what happened? Did you fight? The journalists tell me you two had a very hard meeting!" I saved all the newspapers clips from the next day. Obviously, the information they published did not reflect what had happened.

I met few people who used the media as effectively as Carlos Bianchi. Many sports journalists often mix their personal ideological positions, often aligned with populism, with duty to inform. It is a typical occurrence in soccer and a frequent practice in politics as well. Some interpretations of that time seemed to suggest the idea that

Boca had been successful "despite" our administration. In reality, it was quite the opposite. We had secured the necessary conditions for success to happen through a transformation of the club that was unprecedented in its history.

Once again, I found myself having to choose a new coach for Boca's first team. This time, I acted very quickly. On that same Monday, I spoke with Miguel Ángel Brindisi, and on Tuesday, we reached an agreement that I announced immediately. I remembered an old phrase from adventure novels that I used to read in my childhood: "The King is dead! Long live the King!" Interregnums without leadership often bring enormous dangers to leadership. It was necessary to send a clear signal and put an end to Bianchi's new era, once again putting Boca and its institutional and sporting continuity above all else. Without a doubt, Bianchi's great success meant enormous pressure. But Boca was more important than individuals, and the victories obtained were not an obstacle for the team to continue winning championships and cups in the following years.

Brindisi's tenure was brief, and it was tough for me to accept his resignation after a series of poor results in the local tournament. Miguel had presented his resignation to me twice before, and I rejected it both times. As I have said before, I believe in cycles. However, there came a point when he decided that it no longer made sense to continue, and he resigned for the last time in the locker room after a defeat against River. It was another blow.

At Boca, I learned to understand the coaches' mentalities and the pressure for results that comes both from the stands and from specialized journalism. But my vision was always opposed to this deeply rooted habit in Argentine soccer of changing coaches every time they lose a game. From my perspective as an engineer, planning and consolidating projects are fundamental stages and should not be interrupted. For this reason, I rejected the resignations of Brindisi and so many others time and time again. In my years as a business, I developed a very clear conviction that I maintain to this day: contracts are meant to be fulfilled. Whether in business, soccer, or politics, agreements and one's word have a higher value than anything else. It is a matter of convictions and is beyond discussion.

At that moment, I received a call from Maradona. It was a call that filled me with joy. It had been a long time since that bitter meeting at Luis Conde's house. Diego had been very harsh with me in countless interviews. But for my part, I had learned to let go of anything resembling resentment. Diego was in top form and seemed to have recovered. I felt that the time had come to fulfill my word, so I offered him the position of team coach. However, his plans were already set elsewhere, and a few months later, we would see him become a great TV show host.

We met twice at his home in Villa Devoto. I wanted to find a way to bring Maradona closer to Boca and offered him the vice presidency of the soccer commission, but it didn't work out. Then Diego made a great recommendation: Alfio Basile. I took his advice and discovered in Coco Basile a born leader. His leadership has a different style. His authority does not come from giving orders. On the contrary, his main virtue is an incredible ability to downplay the unbearable tensions that high-level competition carries.

Basile is a calm man. His authority is nourished by the trust he builds with his players. He speaks little, but enough to ensure that the group functions harmoniously. His leadership style is more like mine. He always expressed his willingness to mix the most experienced talents with the youngest ones. Coco transmitted security. He did not let himself be wrapped up by the interests of the media. He was a man from another time, adapted to the present. Under his guidance, that year we won all the championships we played. When he left to coach the national team, his farewell was profoundly moving. We all learned a lot from Coco.

We appointed Ricardo La Volpe as his replacement, who started off badly. Boca was first in the league and ready to win the 2006 Torneo Apertura, several points ahead of the team behind us, yet three consecutive losses and a failed final against Estudiantes de La Plata left us out of the title race. La Volpe's style was practically the direct opposite of Basile's. Outgoing and controversial, he struggled to deal with conflicts. Boca definitely needed another type of coach.

Once again, I faced the same dilemma: a more showmanship-oriented personality who felt the fans' anxiety or a professional capable of sustaining a work program beyond the pressures. I had to prevent the work we had capitalized with Bianchi and Basile from falling apart. Miguel Ángel Russo was the right man. I had considered the possibility of calling Miguel on other occasions, but it had not worked out for different reasons.

Miguel's arrival coincided with the return of Riquelme, who was then in conflict with Villarreal, in Spain. Oscillations and ups and downs are a central characteristic of Román's personality. His return to the team was one of the boldest ideas I had during my time at Boca. We took advantage of the Spanish club's discomfort with Román and paid the sum of $2 million to have him for just four months. It may sound absurd, but it was an investment that paid enormous dividends. The emotional shock was immense for the entire team and also for the fans. I knew it was necessary to make a significant impact, so we could preserve the winning mystique we had from the Bianchi era. I believe that Román felt a deep need to prove that his qualities as a player were still intact after the setback at Villarreal. Thus, with a brilliant Riquelme in top form, we were able to win the 2007 Copa Libertadores.

Riquelme returned and was the standout player of the team. His attitude, unlike what had happened in the previous cycle, made the difference. Román wanted to stay in Boca, but we had no way of paying him what he asked for. Once again, institutional responsibility prevailed. Seeing Riquelme's subsequent downfall, I still think it was a wise decision. Now that he has become a soccer executive, I see the same tensions that he caused during his time as a player.

That Copa Libertadores was the last trophy won during my tenure. It marked the beginning of the end of a chapter in the history of Boca and an unforgettable time in my own life came to an end. We won six titles in the local tournament and ten international cups. Boca lifted a trophy sixteen times in twelve years. More than that "one title per year" that I had promised in 1995. That idea that had tormented me of being "a non-winning president" had completely vanished.

Looking back, I had renovated and refurbished the stadium, put the club's finances in order, built the youth academy headquarters in Casa Amarilla, created the museum, established a new mechanism to finance player purchases such as the investment fund, reformed the bylaws to adapt them to the new century, and many other extraordinary changes. Boca was the manifestation of a very deep conviction. No institution can sustain itself over time without financial solidity. As I have written before, thanks to Palermo's goals, I was able to achieve the passage of a unique measure in Argentine soccer: that the directors back the economic decisions they make at the club with their own personal assets.

We put the Boca colors at the top of the world. We were the vehicle of joy and happiness for millions of fans in Argentina. We had won it all.

The small but influential world of soccer slowly began to recognize what I had done in Boca. I couldn't help but smile when many of those who had fought and criticized me so much spoke of the great work with the youth teams, the modernization of the club, the insertion of Boca into the world, and the meticulousness in the administration. What had happened? The answer is simple: we had won. Once again, I could evoke that wise verse from Rudyard Kipling in his poem "If—" and confirm all its truth when it says: "If you can meet with Triumph and Disaster / And treat those two impostors just the same."

Amid all these overlapping feelings, I could see the end of a vital cycle. I was no longer the same person I was twelve years earlier. Like Boca, I had also grown. I had to capitalize on all that growth.

The first hint that my cycle was ending was when I strangely started to feel like a slave to Boca. I knew then, as I know now, that there is a moment when you have to step aside for others to continue their journeys with their mistakes and successes. I needed to become a fan like everyone else. To shout from the stands like I had done when I was a child.

Soccer is a team game. Perhaps words cannot fully define the meaning of this phrase. I achieved what I achieved in those twelve years because of the team on the pitch and the one that accompanied me in management. Each and every one of them played their part in this story.

Soccer lives in the locker rooms. In the intimacy of the group, amid the smell of liniment, in the steam of the showers, and in the players' codes. The locker room is the most important place in a club. Success or failure is played out there, as much or more than on the pitch. There, the coach constructs a truth that is as valuable for soccer as it is for companies or politics: the team is above any individual.

There may be stars, superstars, geniuses, highly talented players. But nothing happens if the rest of the team does not support it. Everything is mixed in the locker room: injuries, suspensions, internal conflicts, vanities, negative leadership, narcissism. Nothing different from what I later saw in politics. Perhaps in soccer there is more innocence. Perhaps in politics there is more cynicism. But what is at stake is exactly the same. The collective project above the individual project. One for all and all for one.

As the president of Boca, I would always go down to the locker room to greet each player before every game. I wanted to convey my respect, support, and trust. If they were wearing the Boca jersey, it was because they were at the pinnacle of their game. However, I never went down to the locker room after the games. My presence at that moment was always unnecessary. It's a moment of intimacy that must be preserved. Except, of course, after the 3–0 win against River, when Palermo scored that unforgettable goal that stopped time in the universe.

I met many coaches. I respected them all equally. For a leader, support is key. I did it later as mayort and as president. My responsibility is to provide them with the greatest tranquility, confidence, security, and freedom so that each one can do their job well. It sounds obvious. But it's not, neither in soccer nor in politics.

Everyone thinks they are a coach, just as we all think we're economists or presidents. But nobody knows it all. Talking to the different coaches I accompanied, I also learned to listen. I always kept close contact with them and never wanted to transmit pressure; on the contrary, I have always wanted to dissipate it. I loved sitting with them and hearing their visions about the matches, about the players' performance, and from that place—and only from that place—I contributed what I could to achieve what was best for the team.

I learned that choosing the players is the club's prerogative, not that of the coaches. The coach has a limited responsibility. Under his leadership, the team may win or lose but in the long or short run, he will leave. The president, on the other hand, is governed by another logic: the vote. And he has a time-limited mandate. My obsession was always in caring for that material and immaterial heritage called Boca. To make it grow. I tried to do that, and I believe, without false modesty, that I often achieved it.

Soccer gave me so much, and I also gave it a lot. Saying good-bye was dreadful. I couldn't leave, yet I knew I had to step down as president of my beloved club. At that moment, I thought I would never experience anything like it again. Such an intense and significant *what for.*

Once again, I was mistaken.

PART TWO

Power

The City and the Nation

12

Chance and Causality

Leadership and power always go hand in hand. As is the case with leadership, power also holds mysteries and dangers. On one hand, it is a wonderful tool for doing things and transforming reality. On the other, it can destroy you if you are not well-grounded. Over the years, I have seen how desperate many people become about having, accumulating, and conquering power. The temptation to consider power as the ultimate goal in life is enormous for many. But power cannot be an end. It is merely a means.

The issue of power has been present in my family. My father, an Italian immigrant who arrived in Argentina at nineteen, had a very particular relationship with the exercise of power, both within the family and with his collaborators in his companies. Owner of a superior intelligence and an enormous capacity for work, he could simultaneously be generous, arbitrary, and even cruel with those around him. By the time of my kidnapping, Dad had become the number one businessman in Argentina. It was through him that I learned about the best and worst that power can do to people.

Over time, Dad changed and the same effort he put into building a great economic empire later led him toward the destruction of many of his accomplishments. As the eldest son, I witnessed firsthand his rise and decline. I saw him reach the highest peak and descend from there to the bottom. Unintentionally, my father was the best possible example regarding the care and precautions one must have with power. Like all parents, he was a teacher to me but I also had to learn to distance myself from his influence. From an early age, I understood that my relationship with power should be different from his.

Abraham Lincoln is credited with a wise quote: "Nearly all men can stand adversity, but if you want to test a man's character, give him power." The exercise of power brings out the most extraordinary and the most perverse human traits.

Sometimes power can be a drug, a poison for which one must generate one's own antidotes. The main one is to know yourself as much as possible. It may sound like a cliché, but it is not. Only those who know themselves very well can coexist with power without breaking. It is vital to clearly understand one's own weaknesses and flaws in order to be alert and prevent them from taking over one's life.

Against the traps of power, family is another antidote. Love is at the forefront of everything else. Our most intimate personal world, our partner, our children, our lifelong friends. They are the ones who are not intimidated by power because they treat you as they always have. They are the ones who never give up and who will always want to beat me at sports or when playing cards. Power should be kept out of our relationships with our loved ones. There is no public persona in front of them. You are just one of them, without privileges or protocol. They demand that you remain the same person you have always been. That small circle of significant people we are connected to through love is the best aid in keeping our feet on the ground.

Boca was my great leadership school, but it was also my school in politics. It was where I learned that change is possible. At Boca, I began to understand how power works. Everything I found in the world of soccer, I found again, amplified or distorted, in politics. There, you can also find strongmen, intrigues, cliques, conflicts, egos, loyalties, and betrayals. There are good and bad people. There are honest and corrupt ones. There are innocent idealists and cynical pragmatists. But both in soccer and in politics, I found people with an unbreakable commitment to make and change things. These are the best. I surround myself with them as much as I can. They are the ones who work day by day to make transformation a reality.

In the first few months of 1996, I had just been elected to the presidency of Boca. I was still taking my first steps in the club, trying to understand where I was. One afternoon, I received a call from Claudia Bello, who asked to meet with me "to talk about politics," as she explained. Claudia was a young, trusted official of President Carlos Menem. She led a Peronist group in the La Boca neighborhood, was the daughter of a legendary Radical Party leader, Carlos Bello, and headed the Justicialist Party in the City of Buenos Aires. At that time, she was dedicated to attracting people from outside of traditional politics. In fact, she had a decisive influence in the incorporation of another young man, Daniel Scioli, into the ranks of the Justicialist Party, who would go on to win a seat as a national representative the following year.

I met with Claudia Bello during the chaos and enthusiasm of those early times at the club. After chatting for a while about Boca and the country's situation, she asked me if I was willing to be a candidate for mayor of the City of Buenos Aires for the Justicialist Party. That year would see the first election since the city had achieved political autonomy from the national government. "What are you proposing?" I responded, surprised. "I've just been elected president of Boca. It's been my lifelong dream. Also, how would I explain to the people who voted for me that I'm leaving to do something else? Impossible. Forget it," I concluded.

Now it was Claudia's turn to be surprised. She had never seen anyone reject a candidacy. I, on the other hand, never understood those who jump from one place to another, those leaders who can never fully live in the present because they're always focused on their next position.

In 1999, the Peronist party, led by Carlos Menem, made me the same proposal. And once again, I turned it down. My commitment was still with Boca, and we had yet to achieve sporting results to even consider leaving the club.

A year later, Domingo Cavallo launched his own party, Acción para la República, and ran for mayor of Buenos Aires. Although he was no longer part of the government and had distanced himself from Menem, Cavallo had the credentials of having generated the only years of economic stability in the country in decades. He offered me the position of campaign manager, but I declined, despite my admiration for Cavallo's enormous capability. In that election, he ran against Aníbal Ibarra, who defeated him.

In mid-2002, my friend Ramón Puerta shared with me an invitation to have lunch at the Olivos presidential residence from then-president Eduardo Duhalde. Accompanied by Ramón, I went to the presidential residence without imagining that, years later, I would live there for four years. During dinner, Duhalde began to show me a large number of polls. According to the president, the figures indicated with certainty that he was in a position to win the elections scheduled for the following year.

Duhalde had taken office in a traumatic context, following the resignation of Adolfo Rodríguez Saá in the aftermath of the tragic December 2001 events. At that time, the president was desperately looking for a candidate who could defeat his former running mate and now adversary, Carlos Menem. José Manuel de la Sota and Carlos Reutemann had already rejected the same offer that the president was now making to me. Excited, Duhalde promised me the support of part of his party's powerful territorial machine and was hopeful about my eventual presidency. For my part, I listened respectfully and in silence. "So? What do you think?" he asked me when it was time for dessert.

More than once I have wondered what would have happened if I had succeeded in becoming president in 2003 instead of 2015. Of course, it is a conjectural exercise. History cannot be changed. After the great crisis of 2001, everything seemed, paradoxically, simpler. Public spending levels seemed to be under control. At that time, it was 24 percent of GDP. Twelve years of Kirchnerist governments made it soar to an unmanageable 42 percent. At the same time, in 2003, I had not yet gone through the enormous training experience that governing the city meant for me and the enormous team that accompanied me. What was better? Inexperience in a favorable external economic context, that "tailwind" that Kirchnerism had enjoyed in its early days, or accumulating more experience in an adverse context, as would be the case for me starting late 2015 after the disaster of populism? It is a question that has no answer. I took a few seconds to respond to the president, who was observing me, assuming that my answer would be positive. "Eduardo, I truly appreciate that you have thought of me. Maybe you are right and if I accept your proposal, I could win the elections. But my answer is no." Duhalde frowned in disapproval. And I added a phrase that I remember perfectly, "I'm not going to deny that I would like to be president. But I want to get there by causality, not by chance."

The president asked me, "Are you sure? You may not have a second chance."

"It's possible," I replied. "But I will do everything in my power to get there on my own merits when my time comes.

A few days after that meal, Duhalde finally gave his support to the until then almost unknown governor of the province of Santa Cruz, Néstor Kirchner, who would win despite having obtained just over 22 percent of the votes. The reason was that the winner, Carlos Menem, withdrew from the second round fearing a defeat that the polls considered certain.

It was clear that for the political power of the time I was an attractive candidate, and I must admit that I didn't fully understand why. Menem, Cavallo, and Duhalde had huge differences among them. Still, at different times, the three of them approached me, and I had said no to all three. Clearly they saw me as a vehicle to reach a wider audience. My kidnapping in 1991 had made me a well-known person. Later, after my arrival at Boca, my exposure level had grown exponentially. Boca allowed me to enter the homes and be part of conversations of millions of fans and supporters across the country. Although my goal was never to be someone famous and well-known, popularity was a dimension that came with the job.

I am convinced that if I had jumped into politics solely based on my circumstantial fame as president of Boca, I would have risked or even lost the asset that had led me to preside over the club. Leaving Boca at that time would have meant ceasing to be myself, abandoning my dream and passion to be tempted by a logic of power that I do not share. I would have become a tool for the power of others.

Before taking the next step, I had to and wanted to keep my word with those who had brought me to where I was. The popularity that Boca gave me was an important ingredient to make the leap into politics, but it was an insufficient ingredient. Without looking for it, I discovered a fundamental lesson: the levels of knowledge shown in polls do not automatically make a person a good candidate, much less a good leader. In other words, fame is not everything.

The idea of taking my *what for* to politics was already in my head. Someday, I thought, I might try it. Toward the turn of the century, I saw politics as a possible horizon. I needed to learn more to understand what it meant to enter the struggle for real power in society. It was a long process that took time. I had set up a table for political discussion and analysis and I met with its members regularly. Until one day, one of the people who was part of it, sociologist and communications specialist Doris Capurro, put me in touch with Francisco de Narváez and I noticed that we both had similar ideas. Francisco brought along the people who made up the Creer y Crecer Foundation that he had created, and we began working together in their offices on Lafinur Street in the Palermo neighborhood.

The objective of the foundation was to design plans to transform the reality of the City of Buenos Aires and the entire country. I was focused on the city and Francisco on the national project. We regularly met with specialists in the different areas of government who contributed ideas and projects. Creer y Crecer aimed to be what today we would call a think tank, a space that included the participation of prestigious teams of intellectuals, economists, scientists, architects, and urban planners. There was a certain creative effervescence in that foundation. I listened, asked questions, and at the same time discovered new dimensions of the complexity of the nation and public management while becoming increasingly convinced of the need for a change.

In 2003, I felt that after the sporting successes I had had with Boca, I was in a position to end my time at the club and fight my first electoral battle for the position of mayor.

The elections were held on Sunday, August 24, 2003, and my running mate was a young Horacio Rodríguez Larreta, whom I had met through his work leading the Sophia Foundation, which complemented the work we were doing at Creer y Crecer. That day, the Frente Compromiso por el Cambio made its debut in the city. We came in first by a narrow margin over Aníbal Ibarra, who was accompanied by Jorge Telerman representing the then nascent Kirchnerism. The difference in votes was very small. A mere four points separated us from our rivals, which foreshadowed a very contested second round. Behind Ibarra came Luis Zamora and, a little further behind, Patricia Bullrich, the candidate for Unión por Recrear Buenos Aires.

Three weeks later came the runoff and with it, the defeat. Ibarra won with 53 percent of the votes against our front's 47 percent. It was a very tough night. I felt like I had given my all and victory had slipped away from us by very little. I wouldn't be able to carry out my project despite having the support of practically half of the people of Buenos Aires. When I got home that Sunday night, I was destroyed. I cried all night. Defeat is always cruel. I had lost.

However, that first round had resulted in a strong bloc in the legislature with twenty-three representatives. Our ticket had been made up of people who had joined our proposal from different political traditions. But among them, the contribution of a group of new and very young politicians stood out. Possessing an unwavering idealism and a solid academic background, they would make a lot of noise in the following years. They included Gabriela Michetti, Marcos Peña, Soledad Acuña, Paula Bertol, and Martín Borrelli, among others. Their internal rivals soon gave them a derogatory nickname: the "Festilindo" group, after a successful children's music show from the 1980s.

There is something good about defeat. You learn. That low point made me understand, like no other, the importance of values. As had happened in my first campaign for Boca, the formation of Compromiso por el Cambio had been something of an avalanche. We had attracted some traditional and experienced politicians, but also new and healthy leaders who were starting to walk their own paths in politics. My work then and now was the same: to unite. To cradle everyone behind the same dream.

Without an executive position, I had discovered a new role in politics. I wasn't the boss, as I had been in Sideco, nor was I the president, as I had been at Boca. I couldn't give orders. My power now was different. From that moment on, I knew that I would have to lead.

It is essential for the survival of any project to be able to quickly overcome the trauma of defeat. As I have said before, leadership appears during difficult times. Leading in success is easy. The true ability of a leader shows up in the most challenging moments. I had to be able to retain those who had joined us in that first campaign. Now that we had become known, I had to attract others to keep moving forward.

Many thought that after the defeat I would retreat back to soccer or even return to the business world. Some media outlets always underestimated me. They accused me of not having the ability to tolerate an adverse outcome. I was always struck by this. Clearly, they didn't know me.

The morning after the news of the defeat, my tears had already dried up. My cell phone woke me up with a call from an unknown number. "Mauricio, dear!" It was the unmistakable voice of Bambino Veira, with whom I had not spoken since his departure from Boca several years earlier. "I'm calling to tell you that I will never forgive you if you don't press ahead. What you did was extraordinary!"

Some call it resilience. Others simply call it endurance, the ability to tolerate frustration, to tough it out. Whatever its name, it is an essential resource. I had experienced it during the kidnapping and throughout my difficult relationship with my father. I replied to Bambino, "Yes, of course I will press ahead. Whatever happens, we have to keep going." We commented on the results of the previous day and I went to a dentist's appointment I had recently postponed. When I finished, I went straight to the office. I needed to meet my team.

I arrived a little after ten. One by one, they all started to arrive. In them, I saw future ministers, legislators, governors, and officials. They didn't know it yet, but I was convinced that sooner or later it was going to happen.

The few who had already arrived were wandering around not knowing what to do. The election was over. What lay ahead was uncertain. Gradually, the others arrived. I told them that I wanted us all to meet and we squeezed into a room. As the last ones, sad and upset, entered the office, there was a sense of an end to something. As if each one was waking up from a long collective dream and was afraid of having to fend for themselves from that moment on. No more meetings. Each one would return to their own things and the team would inevitably disintegrate. There were also those who had already entered the legislature, some veterans, and others who seemed almost like teenagers.

I wanted to convey to them all the calm and confidence that was possible. I assured them that I was going to continue. "This is just the beginning. We have to keep working together. Now we have a huge responsibility and we cannot let people down. Don't worry; I'll continue to be here and I'll take care of you. Almost half of the people in Buenos Aires voted for us. Cheer up."

Many remember that morning in the office. A very young and timid María Eugenia Vidal asked me, "But who takes care of you?" And I confessed. Since I was very young, I had recognized in my father one of the characteristic traits of power: loneliness. That place where there is no one behind you anymore, and you can only count on yourself.

We had to keep fighting. I wanted that and only that to be my message. We had come to stay. It was about our *what for*, our dreams, the dreams of those who had voted for us. We no longer had the right to give up.

13

Cromañón

The tragedy occurred on the night of December 30, 2004. Some politicians told me that I had been "lucky" not to have won the elections the previous year and not be leading the city government at that time. I have never tolerated the cynicism of the political world. I have always wanted to stay away from people who try to take advantage of anything. Cromañón was not an accident. It was the result of a series of irresponsible practices that existed in the city without anyone having done anything to change them. We had entered politics to eradicate all of that. It was and still is one of our main *what fors*.

Like all Argentines, I felt great pain for each of the 194 people who died that night. It was the first time that I had been in contact with a tragedy of such magnitude. I could identify with the anguish and desperation of the relatives of so many young people who had lost their lives. I also thought that my own children could have been there.

Along with the pain, I saw the fury that had been unleashed against Ibarra and his people and I also felt the enormous pressure of the interests that had come into play after the tragedy. I knew I had a huge responsibility. The parents of the victims had placed on me the obligation to do everything in my power to ensure that the mayor's impeachment could take place. The enormous web of complicity and negligence that made the tragedy possible had to be clear to everyone. I knew it from the start: if that goal was not achieved, the responsibility would be entirely mine. No one else.

Cromañón also called into question the entire political system. This rightfully included some people who were members of our own ranks. When forming our political force, people from all over and from the most diverse backgrounds joined us. Many of them I practically didn't know or had just met a few months ago.

There was talk of incredible economic and political offers being made to some opposition lawmakers with the aim of avoiding at all costs the initiation of the impeachment process and with it, the eventual removal of the mayor. There was a very serious moral issue at stake. Politics and politicians, in particular each one who had responsibilities in the process, found themselves immediately under the scrutiny of society. None of them could seek to save themselves. Rightfully, the pain of dozens of families was going to prevent it. However, I had my doubts about whether everyone would live up to the role they were going to have to play.

Almost a year after the tragedy, in November 2005, the Accusatory Chamber of the Legislature had to approve the initiation of the impeachment process against Aníbal Ibarra and suspend him from his duties. Nestor Kirchner's then chief of staff, Alberto Fernández, was pressuring the folklorist "Chango" Farías Gómez and Sandra Bergenfeld, who were part of our bloc, to get them to change their vote.

A few hours before that vote, one of the most scandalous events I witnessed in my political career took place. On October 23, 2005, legislative elections had been held. I headed the ticket of candidates for national representatives for Alianza Propuesta Republicana, the direct predecessor of Propuesta Republicana (PRO), accompanied by Paula Bertol in second place and the then well-known doctor and journalist Eduardo Lorenzo "Borocotó," who was in third place followed by another young man who would make headlines, Esteban Bullrich. We did very well and obtained six out of the thirteen seats up for grabs. Behind us came Elisa Carrio's ticket. Kirchnerism, represented by Rafael Bielsa, came in third.

Two years earlier, Borocotó had won a seat as a legislator for the city through our ticket. Until his entry into the House of Representatives, he continued to be part of our bloc in the city legislature. Hours before the session in which the impeachment of Ibarra was to be decided, Borocotó met with Alberto Fernández and Néstor Kirchner at the Casa Rosada for more than an hour and from there announced with great fanfare that he would not be part of the bloc for which he had been elected in Congress. Instead, he had decided to form a single-person bloc allied with Kirchnerism. It was one of the most incredible and shameful cases of political defection in the history of our country. There was total repudiation and condemnation of what Borocotó had done. People witnessed in disbelief the spectacle of betrayal of the trust that had been placed in a politician. Popular wit soon created the neologism "*borocotear*" as a synonym for failing to keep one's word and switching to the rival's side.

After the meeting between Alberto Fernández and Borocotó and given the closeness of the chief of staff with Anibal Ibarra, doubts about the participation and vote of Borocotó and the other two legislators grew exponentially. Nobody knew for sure how they were going to vote. The reaction of the parents of the Cromañón victims was tremendous. Everyone realized how crude the political maneuver had been. There was complete parity. A vote in one direction or the other could change the expected result. Faced with the magnitude of the rejection, Borocotó decided to attend the session. The same happened with Farías Gómez and Bergenfeld, two other uncertain votes.

That was how Alberto Fernández's clumsiness and political cynicism managed to dispel all doubts. When it was time to vote, all of our legislators voted as planned. With those three votes that had generated so much expectation, the thirty necessary votes were obtained to initiate the impeachment process against the mayor.

It was a very important moment in our political history. We needed to clarify the place and importance that the institutions of the city should have. This episode confirmed my intuitions about politics. The same ones that I had taken to Boca. On the one hand, power cannot withstand lies. When a politician degrades his word and changes his speech to suit the pressures he receives, he loses all the credit with his voters. The vote is a contract and, as I have already written, I am one of those who believe that contracts must be fulfilled. On the other hand, I confirmed the enormous value of another voice: that of public opinion. Society can forgive mistakes, but it will never forgive moral breakdown. When integrity is lost, there is no possible return.

Cromañón was a display of the degradation of politics. I admit that the extent of that degradation was a surprise to me. I had known members of the political class for some time. At the end of 2001, society had condemned them, crying out, "They must all go!" But not even in my most pessimistic view could I have imagined what I experienced around a tragedy such as that one.

For many years now, we have been living with this scam, this perverse deformity that is "political correctness." It is a trap under which the incorrect, the wrong, and the things that should not be done are often hidden. Like a true language police, it travels through our minds, protecting those who do not deserve to be protected, limiting our field of action to avoid offending some or disturbing others.

The ruling party at the time had considered it "politically correct" to protect Omar Chabán, the person responsible for Cromañón. Chabán was part of a "progressive" circuit and had friends in power. He operated within a world full of implicit understandings and corrupt practices, which led to his establishment not being properly inspected and failing to meet the essential safety requirements intended to prevent a tragedy like the one that unfortunately occurred.

I remember the messages and visits from the members of the political system of that time. The "caste," as Javier Milei would dub them years later. One after another they approached me to say that it was in my best interest for Ibarra to continue in his position because he was in his second term and would not have the possibility to be reelected. On the other hand, if his deputy mayor, Jorge Telerman, succeeded him, he would have the opportunity to complete the term and then try for another one afterward. Those who supposedly knew about politics encouraged me to go against what I believe in. To my horror, these were not just voices coming from the outside. There were some among our own ranks who held that same theory. I could not believe my ears. I could not, cannot, and will not accept that politics carries that level of alienation and distance from values.

Conviction and convenience are two forces that can work together in the exercise of power. However, convenience cannot come at the expense of conviction. Cromañón put our convictions above anything else. In order to achieve our goals, exemplary behavior was and continues to be nonnegotiable. Fortunately, I found the same conviction in Gabriela Michetti. It was Gaby, through her enormous courage, who took undertook the search for the truth in the legislature.

Cromañón caused me a true and deep pain. Those deaths were as real as they were avoidable. The suffering and anguish shown by those mothers and fathers were as real as their willingness to fight to the end in their demand for justice. Those who wanted to distance me from my convictions to go after a miserable political convenience were wrong. I refused. Time and again, I said no. I knew what was at stake. It seemed tremendous to me that political convenience was capable of questioning why we do what we do; the *what for* behind what we do. They couldn't do it with me. They couldn't get away with it with Gabriela. They couldn't do it with Marcos or with any of those young people who put ethics above convenience from the start. In the face of the use that politics wanted to make of a tragedy, we held our identity at all costs.

The process which followed the Cromañón tragedy made us all grow. People put us in a position that demanded we never give up. It was traumatic, but at the same time it gave us greater robustness. It was a fundamental milestone in our journey. We established a moral boundary that we were never willing to cross.

It was also a decisive moment for me and my conception of leadership and power. Our project consists of developing a better society. If we had contributed to obstructing the investigation into Cromañón, everything would have ended. All our dreams, ideals, and the *what for*, the purpose of my participation would have been buried forever. Society always set a higher standard for us than for other political actors. Our voters would have never forgiven that moral stain. At that moment, the egg hatched. The quest for change had begun.

14

Power and the *What For*

Goar Mestre was one of my great teachers. He was a wise grandfather figure to me whom I always listened to carefully. I was fortunate to cross paths with him in the 1980s. At that time, my father had partnered with the legendary Cuban television producer when he tried unsuccessfully to enter the private TV business.

Goar would always tell me that before adding a person to my team, I should consider their human quality above their technical abilities. "If they're at least fifty-one percent good people, you can work with them. But if they don't exceed forty-nine percent, forget it. Even if they're experts in their field, they won't be of any use to you." Those words were etched into my memory.

In the origins of Compromiso para el Cambio, what would later be known as PRO, people with very diverse characteristics participated. Not everyone had approached our political party for the same reasons. There were veteran politicians who came from different previous experiences and young people who were taking their first steps. In the legislature, they grouped themselves into two blocs. There were the "Nogaró", named after the Buenos Aires hotel where they held their meetings, and the "Festilindo", which brought together many of the emerging leaders from the work carried out at the Creer and Crecer and Sophia foundations. As always, my job was to cradle everyone and separate the wheat from the chaff. Goar's thin boundary line was relentless. Over time, the best were able to find one another, and others were left behind as they did not meet the 51 percent rule.

Not all the support we received in the early days fit the bill. Some who represented traditional politics considered that, due to their history or the knowledge they claimed to have of the political system, they should occupy relevant positions in the party we were founding.

The idea of founding a new party was very audacious. By the turn of the century, our political system was made up of two major traditional forces with many decades of history: the Radical Civic Union and the Justicialist Party. Both parties had gone through times of success and failure, and for better or for worse, they were burdened with the past. On the other hand, I had seen different forces be born and also extinguish which, at various times, had tried to mediate between those giants. In most cases, they were only able to play a testimonial role, unable to express a true vocation for power.

I wasn't entirely sure, but unknowingly I was repeating an old family legend. My father had once told me a story that featured my grandfather, Giorgio Macri, who passed away when I was entering adolescence. Over the years, I was able to discover more about that forgotten tale. After the fall of fascism in Italy, my grandfather had played an important role along with his friend Guglielmo Giannini in the creation of a new political party: Il Partito dell' Uomo Qualunque, the Party of the Common Man, following the success of a satirical newspaper they published under the same name.

My grandfather's party was a staunch opponent of both fascism and communism. It was born out of a strong rejection of traditional parties, proposed a radical reform of the nation, and was a defender of the free market. The Qualunquists, as they were called, performed very well in the first democratic elections in postwar Italy. Dad, still a teenager in Rome, accompanied my grandfather to countless meetings, which was the only partisan involvement I knew of in his life. In 1948, Giorgio Macri emigrated to Argentina, one year before my father did. Shortly after, the Qualunquists began to lose relevance until they disappeared completely. Obviously, something of all that, that dissatisfaction with what was given, ran in my blood. Decades after my grandfather's political experience, I found myself embarking on a similar path.

The PRO was something different from the start. In order to conquer power and carry out the transformations project that I had proposed, I understood that I needed a political force that would express our *what for*. In the eyes of the traditional political system, we always represented a disruptive element. We had decided to compete for power to express change and a radical break with the most traditional forms of Argentine politics.

First and foremost, the PRO is a party composed of good people who share a vocation of service and a set of nonnegotiable values and principles. We form a different, novel, and contemporary identity, often unclassifiable for political analysts. At the same time, we entered politics with an almost obsessive idea of change.

I have said many times that it doesn't matter where each person comes from but where we are all heading together. If we are heading toward an open, democratic, republican society, integrated into the world, with liberal values, striving for progress and development, then we can play on the same team. Diversity made us strong as long as we shared the essential nature of our *what for*, our purpose. As a leader, my role was always to maintain that unity in diversity.

In order to build a real power project, you always have to keep one eye on your convictions and the other on political opportunity. As was my case in those first encounters, before reaching the presidency of Boca, the story of my own history and my own *what for* found resonance and inspired many people to join politics for the first time.

Many people joined driven by the irresistible force of their convictions. Loyal to their principles, they left their comfort zone in the private sector to be part of something bigger and transcendent. It was not about my personal project but about a project of change that went beyond individuals. Others, on the other hand, joined out of convenience and opportunism, leaving their convictions relegated to a second consideration. In general, sooner or later, they left. I have always felt more comfortable in the field of convictions. Loyalties that arise from common ideas are always the most enduring in a territory as fragile as that of politics.

The lesson is that power is built with what we have. Sometimes we have to do it with the good ones and with those who are not so good. We couldn't make a party with a vocation for power by importing political leaders from Sweden or Finland. We had to do it with those who were willing. And at the same time, I had to carry out a dedicated teaching task so that, once again, everyone was very clear about why and with what purpose we were seeking power. From the beginning, I chose generosity and offered spaces for everyone to be a protagonist. That was always my strategy to maximize the commitment and growth potential of everyone who joined.

In the United States, there is an expression that represents me completely in the difficult task of building a new political party. They have this idea of "learning by doing." I had to learn by doing. It happened to me in the companies I worked for, it happened to me again in Boca, and it happened once more when I entered politics. I had to learn how to lead in diversity—a tremendously diverse group of people whom I practically did not know. I had to make them believe in me and be able to transmit to each one what we were doing. It was a path that was not without mistakes. Many times I had to swallow my pride to keep agreements. I learned to deal with huge egos and narcissism. It was not easy. On more than one occasion, I had to bite my tongue. Political leadership does not consist of seeing who shouts the loudest. On the contrary, anger is always useless. In a company, you give orders. In politics, you lead and persuade. In a democracy, it is the votes which give way to political order. Learning by doing was the best method toward doing what we did and getting where we got.

In 2005, I was elected as a national representative for the City of Buenos Aires. For someone like me, whose passion lies in doing, working as a legislator was not particularly stimulating. The idea of my candidacy arose from a strategy aimed at helping the growth and consolidation of our political force. In this sense, the electoral campaign opened up the possibility of bringing my message to society as a whole.

Once I had taken my seat, I soon realized that I was in the wrong role. I found myself facing the limitations of a very small and ultra-minority bloc in the face of a Kirchnerism representation that already had a comfortable majority of its own. We could barely fulfill a testimonial and declarative function. Due to its own function in our system, Congress is far from the executive function. The legislative labyrinths and our almost zero impact sometimes resulted in losing sight of the objectives in the face of the weight of what Emilio Monzó once defined as "the rosca," that constant negotiation, that classic give and take of the legislative environment. The representative position was definitely not for me.

Those two years in Congress coincided with the end of my time at Boca. The year 2007 was a new turning point in the history of our project and in my own life.

15

I Do Not Regret this Love

It was 2007 and, for the second time, I was a candidate for mayor of the City of Buenos Aires. In response to my candidacy, the ruling Kirchnerism Party had launched an aggressive campaign aimed at discrediting me. Their slogan was "Mauricio is Macri." As a good populist, Néstor Kirchner operated based on his own prejudices and believed that society would be willing to act according to his aggressiveness and simplifications.

Sunday, June 3, was a special day. A crowd of people had entered the corner café on Santa Fe Avenue and Scalabrini Ortiz to greet me and wish me good luck in the elections. As I tried to make my way through a swarm of journalists, onlookers, and supporters, before casting my vote at the school across the street, an elderly woman approached me and said she wanted to tell me something important. I stopped to listen as she looked me in the eyes and said, "Mauricio, be yourself. Whatever happens, please always be yourself."

That day the people of Buenos Aires went to the polls to elect a new mayor. The period that had begun with Aníbal

Ibarra and continued with Jorge Telerman was coming to an end. I was accompanied on the ticket by a young politician with extraordinary charisma. Her name was Gabriela Michetti. Gaby had won a seat in the city's legislature in 2003, and as I have mentioned, played a decisive role in the aftermath of the Cromañón tragedy. Little by little, she became increasingly popular. I was convinced that her charm and intelligence were destined to reach the hearts of the people of Buenos Aires. She represented the change we were proposing like few others.

That Sunday our ticket prevailed over the Kirchnerist ballot headed by Daniel Filmus and Carlos Heller, doubling it in votes. We got over 47 percent but we had to go to a runoff three weeks later. We obtained more than one million votes, representing 61 percent of the total votes cast.

That night I felt immense happiness. The traditional political world always had a hard time understanding and accepting our joy. I remember myself in the bunker dancing with Gabriela from her wheelchair among yellow balloons while Gilda's voice came out of the speakers saying what I myself felt: "I do not regret this love." The dancing, the balloons, and the happiness we were experiencing and expressing were elements that only spurred indignation in our rivals, too accustomed to always coloring politics with a strong, dramatic tone.

We have always challenged that bitter paradigm. Over the years, our way of campaigning and celebrating our victories would be copied by the same political sectors that since 2007 questioned and placed joy on the same level as frivolity.

I never knew why I danced with Gabriela that night. It was a spontaneous way of showing my joy. Dancing is a shared act. Being myself, as that lady had asked me weeks before, requires naturalness, freshness, truth. That's what it's all about. Like anxiety or sadness, joy cannot be simulated or hidden. I was happy because we had come a long way. Time had passed, we had grown. But the most important question remained: Would we be able to fulfill what we had proposed to the people of Buenos Aires?

Once the celebrations, the dances, and the balloons were left behind, it was time to assemble the team to go out to the field. One thing was theory and quite a different one was practice. For the position of chief of staff, I chose Horacio Rodríguez Larreta. Horacio had approached me years before with the team of the Sophia Foundation. From there, he worked on the design of government plans across different areas. It was through him that young professionals, such as María Eugenia Vidal, Carolina Stanley, or Eugenio Burzaco, approached our team.

Unlike me, Horacio came from a family that had been involved in politics for several generations. He himself had extensive experience in public administration. He had served as a government official during Domingo Cavallo's tenure as Minister of Economy and in the area of social development alongside Palito Ortega. He had gained some renown as comptroller at PAMI (Programa de Atención Médica Integral, a public health insurance agency) during the presidency of Fernando de la Rúa, and in 2003, had run with me as the candidate for deputy mayor. We have been working together ever since.

I always found it easy to work with Horacio. Unlike many political leaders, he is a person with a strong control over his ego who places great importance on efficiency. He is someone with an enormous capacity for work and organization. The dynamic with which I had envisioned the role of the chief of staff made it necessary for me to devote a lot of time during my first term to empowering him in front of the other ministers. I needed the chief of staff to be able to build his own authority over the rest of the team and to be able to exercise it autonomously.

In companies, organizational charts usually define vertical lines of command. There are bosses and subordinates. Today, this is being discussed and transformed by more horizontal schemes. But there is always someone above, with greater decision-making power, whether it is the shareholder, the CEO, or the general manager. In politics and public management, things are different.

Among those who join a political project, egos play a decisive role. Although everyone shares a basic agreement in the realm of ideas, it is common for some to perceive themselves above others and find it difficult or uncomfortable to accept subordination. Throughout our history, at PRO we have been able to successfully resolve this type of situation. In other more traditional political forces, the issue of authority is experienced differently and internal disputes often reach gigantic proportions that end up destroying any form of organization.

This is why I always empowered the role of chief of staff. In my political power architecture within the administration, it is a key role so that individual responsibilities are not diluted. The chief of staff is not just another minister. My idea is that it is a position that calls for the coordination of the ministers' work and assessment of the degree of project fulfillment. Of course, it was a substantial change and not something that ministers and officials could easily accept. What is a normal process in a company was an enormous amount of work in the city government.

This method was a revolution in the way the city was managed, which I later brought to the nation. The follow-up meetings with each minister and their team, the implementation of the dashboard with alerts through which indicators could quickly indicate the degree of goal compliance, the extended cabinet meetings with the participation of second and third lines, and the cabinet meetings themselves were largely responsible for having been able to carry out the number of transformations we succeeded in implementing.

Managing dissent is another major challenge in exercising power. It is a central issue in any activity and has a crucial impact. To address it, I decided from the beginning of my political career to have a small group that the press dubbed the "inner circle." It is a trusted group intended for discussion and debate on possible courses of action.

This type of reflective space for decision-making is of great importance and requires a lot of active listening on the part of the leader.

This inner circle has helped me avoid mistakes and has also been behind numerous successes. The dynamics of this space require deep intellectual honesty from all its members. The leader must guarantee freedom to express diverse and even contrary opinions to their own. At the same time, they must be willing to follow the majority's opinions. Ultimately, the responsibility for decisions always falls on the leader. However, at the same time, group members must have the necessary courage to resist the temptation to please, even at the cost of difficult or tough discussions. As I have said before, the main problem in exercising power always lies in the ego. If family and friends have always been two of my main antidotes to the dangers of power, the inner circle was the third. It is a fundamental element toward making the best decisions.

In the the city government, I appointed Marcos Peña as secretary general. Marcos had joined the Creer y Crecer Foundation as a junior when he was in his early twenties. From the beginning, his voice was different from others and he made himself noticed. Marcos thinks differently. He has a superior strategic ability and from very early on, he understood the decisive role that communication played in the power project we were building. In a way, he was responsible for turning our *what for* into a strategy. He understood before anyone else that the meaning of what we were doing required enormous work on proximity and connection with residents. Marcos saw the value of the then-new social media and the cultural changes they brought about. He was one of the ideologists of change and one of the gateways for many other young people like him who felt represented in the transformation we were undertaking.

Among the dangers and risks involved in exercising power is self-complacency. Power tends to attract people who cope with their insecurity by always saying yes. Power creates a sort of aura of infallibility in its wielder that is completely false and destructive. In my father's companies, people used to talk about "yesfracism." It was the way of defining the actions of those managers who were incapable of standing by their own criteria and who avoided offering their points of view when Dad presented one of his many crazy projects.

The idea that everyone agrees with you can be attractive to those who use power to reassert themselves. But that comfort inevitably generates the worst results. It is essential to always have intelligent people who stand by their own criteria and ideas. Marcos was someone who fulfilled that role perfectly. Unlike those who say yes to everything, Marcos always offered his vision on every topic at all times. This is not a minor matter. The leader has a sort of moral obligation to always listen. No one, not even the most brilliant of leaders, is infallible.

To build my first government team, I called upon various individuals who did not come from politics. I was as convinced then as I am now that there are no possibilities for real change if only those who have been trained in the culture we are seeking to transform are favored. Carrying out our *what for* requires always calling upon the best. It is what I have sought to do from the beginning.

16

Initial Inconsistency and Its Risks

I am not afraid of risk. I know that you can win or lose when taking risks, but you cannot win if you do not take them. Rational calculations and dispassionate technical analyses are essential for decision-making. The bad news is that, despite everything, they are insufficient. Every decision is accompanied by a set of variables whose behavior we do not know. It is impossible to know in advance what will happen with this or that, what others will do, or what the evolution of the trends manifesting in the present will be. At the time of formulating a strategy, all these elements play a leading role. However, I insist, it is not enough.

On the other hand, when intuition is the only guide, the danger lies in improvisation, one of the worst methods for leading and exercising power. Analysis and preparation serve to minimize risks. My best decisions have always been the result of the sum of all these aspects: reason and passion, brain and heart, analysis and conviction. They were all crucial to carry out my *what for*.

At times, life moves forward smoothly and progressively, but at certain moments, progress occurs through jumps and more abrupt changes. When I review my own path, I find that time and again these changes occurred once I had mastered the fear of the risks that they entailed. Leading a company, presiding over Boca, heading the city government with a new political force, and especially reaching the country's presidency in a context of great weakness, were decisions not exempt from enormous threats and risks.

From a rational and utilitarian point of view, one could think that all those decisions were taken without considering the dangers that they could entail. However, I took them because my *what for* has always been stronger than the risk and its possible consequences.

In that sort of unconsciousness, in that leap into the unknown, in that liberating detachment lies the necessary strength to reach great goals. The relationship between consciousness and audacity is a central tension in the exercise of power. Too much prudence can carry an even greater risk than the unconsciousness required, in many cases, to decide to shake things up and break inertia, thus generating the conditions for change.

There is no single moment of decision-making in the face of risk. There is no brilliant enlightening moment that leads one to make a bold decision. Decisions mature over personal evolutionary processes until one day they manifest in concrete actions. This logic was repeated in every step I have taken throughout my life.

The main decisions I have made share a common factor: leaving my comfort zone to move to another where I had to start building myself again from scratch. It is true that there were elements of my education and business experience that were hugely useful when I arrived at Boca. I have already written that Boca was my degree into politics, and much of what I learned there influenced my work as mayor of the City of Buenos Aires. And my experience there was of great value to my presidency later. In any case, each step led me to a new beginning.

An aversion to risk is incompatible with making things happen. To transform reality, it is necessary to go beyond calculation and speculation. How many times did I have to go against what others told me? How many prejudices did I have to face? I heard the same warnings so many times! "It's not possible", "It's never been done," "You won't succeed," "No one has ever achieved that," almost always spoken with the best of intentions. Despite that, my internal drive led me to try it beyond the obstacles that arose, which were not few.

Transforming a large construction company like Sideco into a service provider was unthinkable. Incorporating a capitalist paradigm into the culture of Boca and Argentine soccer was something profoundly disruptive and it required a lot of politics in the best sense of the term; that is, building alliances and agreements to make a shared project a reality.

Creating a new political party from scratch with the capacity to compete and govern in a country where the major parties were born many decades ago was another bold move, a leap without a safety net that made me go beyond what was expected and grow. Almost all attempts to have third forces against the traditional weight of Peronism and Radicalism ended in failure or were forgotten.

In companies, relationships are established based on an employment contract. In politics, it is a different type of contract, based on ideas. That is why I always sought to build diverse and heterogeneous teams that could minimize the dimension of risks. When I see how officials are shuffled around and replaced without knowing if the new ones have the necessary expertise, experience, and capability, I am increasingly convinced of the importance and centrality of work teams. Individual will is always insufficient. Always.

Not fearing risk was a key element from the beginning. Knowing that things could go wrong was never a hindrance. When I started at Boca, I had my fears. I thought that my inexperience could play against me. However, over time I realized that the madness, the pressure, and the demand to do my job well guided me more toward success than failure.

I have never been interested in achieving a position for the position itself. I did not want to become the president of Boca just to hold the position. I wanted to change Boca, I wanted to change the club and Argentine soccer. The same thing happened to me in the city and in the nation. I never had that obsession so common among public figures of staying tied to power through the nation. I was never interested in getting there to be part of that political "caste" that is so often talked about. I prefer the rotation between the private sector, the academic world, and politics. It is a more beneficial path for society and also for individuals. The formation of closed, endogamous systems is not validated in positive results. Those who promote these systems are usually more concerned with their own preservation than with the transformations for which they felt called upon in the first place.

I was never willing to negotiate that initial recklessness, the vocation for change above all else. Obviously, I am not the same person I was in Sideco in my twenties, nor am I the one who was thirty-six when he became president of Boca. I am no longer even forty-eight, which was my age when I was elected by the people of Buenos Aires as their mayor. The omnipotence I felt at the beginning of my career gave way to a humbler feeling. In the end, it is always about the same thing: resisting the fear of failure, the most paralyzing aspect for a leader.

That sense of recklessness is part of my identity. Maturity brought on an additional tool. It provided me with an enormous wealth of accumulated experiences and lessons learned. However, maturity should never become a burden that ends up canceling out the spirit of change. It is about living with an understanding of the functioning of the present without false nostalgia. The greatest risk of not taking risks is becoming anachronistic. The more leaders they move further away from risk and change, the more they age. In other words, the further they get from that initial fire.

Leading in twenty-first-century politics is more complex than it was in the recent past. The technological revolution has empowered citizens in ways we have never seen before. The massive access to information through the digital universe has brought countless benefits to society but, at the same time, it has generated a state of constant dissatisfaction and anxiety.

After the end of my term, I had the opportunity to talk at length about what I call "the revolution of expectations" with the president of France, Emmanuel Macron. We agreed that the Yellow Vest protests that shook his country from 2018 onward was an example of this true revolution without leaders or precise programs.

This type of popular reactions has taken place in different countries and under governments of different political parties. All of them resulted from important events but are unable to explain the dimension of the mobilizations that they unleashed. In France, it was about an increase in fuel prices. In a very short time, the demands spread chaotically, without clear leadership and accumulating disparate demands. It happened violently in Chile due to an increase in transportation fares at the end of President Piñera's term in office, in Colombia due to a tax reform, and also in the United States after the killing of an African American citizen by police forces. In all cases, the dynamics were similar.

In this world of increasingly complex realities, society appears to be determined to tell its leaders, time and again, "We want more!" The infinite access to information and instant communication in today's world poses a completely new scenario. It is, undoubtedly, the greatest challenge to power that has emerged in recent years. The fate of democratic order will depend on how we can face and solve these new challenges.

17

"Mauricio, Don't Say It Will Continue to Flood"

"We're going to do it. But you must do it in one hundred and eighty days. One hundred and eighty, not a single day more! Is that clear?" Daniel Chain and Guillermo Dietrich looked at me terrified. Daniel was the Minister of Urban Development. Guillo served as Undersecretary of Transportation. I had called them to listen to the opinions of Santiago de Estrada, one of the main critics of the idea of building the Metrobus on the 9 de Julio Avenue, the wide avenue that crosses the city, connecting the neighborhoods of Retiro and Constitución.

"This is not going to work," Santiago repeated, shaking his head. De Estrada was not the only one opposed to the project. Several members of my cabinet shared his views. Some told me directly that I had gone crazy. They couldn't understand why I would create such a traffic mess in the middle of the city; they said people were going to get angry and never vote for us again.

In May 2011, we had inaugurated the first Metrobus on Juan B. Justo Avenue. We had not invented anything. The concept was successfully being implemented in some important cities around the world under the name BRT or Bus Rapid Transit. It is an efficient alternative intended to streamline public transportation through exclusive lanes and stops.

In the face of all the criticism and fears, the technical teams planned the jobs in great detail. We didn't improvise, we studied. I listened with respect to all the adverse opinions. I was aware that we had to minimize disruption to the neighbors, and that is why I decided to limit the construction time to those one hundred and eighty days. I had one certainty: being able to build the 9 de Julio Metrobus in due time and manner was a way to show society and ourselves that we were capable of changing the country.

The Metrobus project is a precise example of my idea of power as a tool for change. I used my power to tilt the balance toward action, toward our *what for*. I decisively supported Guillo and his team's commitment and enthusiasm; I knew that the only way they were going to be able to rise to the challenge was with my full support. They achieved it and by doing so, forever changed the way we move through the city center.

What we didn't imagine at that time was that shortly thereafter, the 9 de Julio Metrobus would become a symbol of everything we did in the City of Buenos Aires. It wasn't the first or the last transformation I undertook, but it was the one that had the most impact on the real meaning of change. Few exemplified so clearly where *what for* lay: the Metrobus offers enormous economic advantages, in terms of reducing pollution and improving urban infrastructure. But there is one improvement that is above all others: time. The Metrobus reduced travel time along 9 de Julio Avenue by 40 percent. For commuters, that translates into several hours less per month on the bus. According to the most serious estimates, the Metrobus made it possible for Buenos Aires residents traveling from the downtown Bajo area to Constitución to recover seven days per year.

Over time, the system was extended to numerous neighborhoods in Buenos Aires, the metropolitan area, and in different cities throughout the country. Still, the work on the second Metrobus, the one on 9 de Julio Avenue, had something special. It was a risky bet like few others. Among its promoters was Daniel Chain, whom I met when we were both very young. Daniel was the first winner of the Socma Scholarship, that great initiative my father created to attract the best young professionals who had just graduated from university. From the start of our work at Creer y Crecer, Daniel coordinated the transformation projects of the city alongside a multidisciplinary team. Once we were elected, he was responsible for turning those countless ideas into tangible realities for the city residents.

He was in charge of enormous transformations. He took on the challenge of restoring the Colón Theater and carried out historic reforms in the neighborhoods, particularly in the southern area of the city. He designed and executed a cutting-edge project, the pedestrianization of the Microcentro, which forever changed an area that was practically uninhabitable, with narrow sidewalks and streets crowded with cars and buses, into a project ahead of its time that valued a key area of the city.

I had another doer on the team. I remember that two years into the the city government's term, Esteban Bullrich told me that he wanted me to meet with one of the young people who had approached the G25, a group we had created to invite professionals from the private sector to participate in public management. "Guillermo Dietrich," Esteban replied when I asked who it was. His name rang a bell from the time I worked in the automotive industry. "He's an extraordinary guy and he's very eager to join." That's how Guillo came to be in the city government when he was just forty years old.

I can't recall how we chose the transportation area for him. He had no experience in it beyond his work at his family's car dealership. What I do know is that he had a special drive. An extraordinary desire to do new things. I immediately realized that his boldness and daring spirit would contribute greatly to our project. I was not mistaken. Guillo undertook some emblematic projects, such as the Metrobus and the city's bike lane system, among others.

During this process, a problem arose. Daniel and Guillo's styles couldn't have been more different. The former brought solid academic training and experience, while the latter was pure enthusiasm. Both worked very well, but they had trouble understanding each other. For me, it was another leadership challenge. How could I get the best out of both without losing either one? I knew that they both had so much to give despite their differences. After thinking about it for a while, I concluded that I needed to change Guillo's reporting line, so he then started reporting to the chief of staff instead of to Chain. The solution worked:

from the word go, Guillo got along perfectly with Horacio. It is essential for organizations to be flexible enough to adapt to the different work characteristics and modalities of those who are part of them. The idea of separating them worked as a buffer for the differences between Guillo and Daniel, and both were able to perform more comfortably from then on. Internal tensions can cause enormous damage. Avoiding them is another responsibility that falls upon the leader.

Few things were more irritating for Buenos Aires residents than seeing the circulation space for their cars reduced. There came a point where it seemed like Guillo was possessed, creating bike lanes across all neighborhoods, especially in the city center. One of the most contentious ones was on Montevideo Street. Guillo pushed to keep it, while others screamed to eliminate it. Guillo remained inflexible and made an intelligent decision. He proposed touring the area together by bike. I remember we were shouting from one bike to the other as we tried to have a conversation.

We had started the program in late 2007. We had still not finished building the first sixty miles of bike lanes, but a significant number of cyclists riding around the city were already visible. Guillo's main argument was that if we gave up on one bike lane, we would soon end up giving up on others and the plan would unravel until it became irrelevant.

The concept of a sustainable city was central. I learned a lot in the transformation process by seeing how the change in waste management, the new pedestrian areas, changes in traffic circulation, and the Metrobus, were all related to the bike lanes as well.

After riding from one end to the other of the much-debated bike lane, I made the decision to trust Guillo. Trust always generates commitment. The enormous cultural change we were promoting was defined, paradoxically, by that problem. Either the motorists who double parked or directly did so on the bike lane win, or the cyclists and the change would.

Years later, I wonder what would have happened if I had joined the chorus of those who distrusted the public works and had rejected his point of view. Guillo probably would have left his job in the public sector and, with him, we would have lost the driving force behind the revolution of airplanes, trains, roads, and highways, and so many transformations that we undertook together starting in 2015 at the National Ministry of Transportation. It is for things like these that power serves a purpose. The bicycles prevailed, and today the city is a leader and pioneer in the mobility transformation.

I know that sometimes infrastructure projects are seen as something cold and distant. But for those of us who have a true passion for getting things done, projects are very much alive. I believe I inherited this from my father. There are projects that cannot be seen, but they change the lives of thousands and thousands of neighbors.

For decades, floods in different areas of the city were part of the usual landscape. Those who experienced them know very well what it is all about. In a matter of minutes, ground-floor apartments, stores and all their merchandise, houses, basements, and underground garages would all be filled with water. Several times a year, television crews and radios reported on the never-ending dramas of families and store owners who saw no way out.

In 2008, I had to face my first floods as mayor. I wanted to be as realistic as possible and said, "Look, we're going to do a project on the Maldonado stream. It will be a very important project, the most significant one since the stream was intubated seventy years ago. When the next storm comes, it will flood again and it will also flood again next year. It will continue to flood in two years and in three years as well, but when we finish, it will never flood again."

I was heavily criticized from the political spectrum. Who in their right mind announces that a problem will continue to exist? "Mauricio, don't say that it will continue to flood!" they said angrily. For the system, a politician must lie, deny reality, promise something they know they won't fulfill. That's no longer acceptable.

Traditional politics tends to think that water infrastructure works do not result in votes, that they are not visible, and that, to make matters worse, they take a long time. It is the short-term vision of power. According to this view, so entrenched in populism, the rule is that no infrastructure projects should be initiated if there is a chance they may be inaugurated in another term, by another mayor or president. I have seen the national government that succeeded me inaugurate numerous works without even mentioning that they had begun during our administration. Similarly, I saw them reversing extremely important projects, such as the gas pipeline that was supposed to transport the gas extracted in Vaca Muerta. I find this selfishness on behalf of a good part of the political class incomprehensible.

In August 2019, I remembered this story. We had fought and worked hard to be able to carry out the project on the Vega and Maldonado streams, as well as so many others. That is why I suddenly forgot that I was in the middle of closing the presidential campaign and I let loose and shouted at the top of my lungs, "No more damn floods!" At that moment, I felt like I was facing all those politicians who did not understand and still do not understand the w*hat for* behind power. Our *what for*, our purpose remains the same: transformation, change, no matter what happens or who is bothered by it.

18

The Power of Symbols

I don't know exactly how many times I have made the journey between Tandil, where I was born, and Mar del Plata. Ever since I was a child, I came and went on countless occasions. Every time I cover those miles, I do the same ritual: to stop by the side of road and buy a Balcarce dessert. Those who know me are familiar with my sweet tooth and the Balcarce dessert—its combination of sponge cake, whipped cream, marron glacé, nuts, dulce de leche, and meringue is one of the most delicious things I have ever tried. I have loved it since I was a child.

After having already been elected mayor of the City of Buenos Aires, one afternoon, I stopped by that small store to buy a dessert for the road, as I had so many times before. I struck up a conversation with the store owners, a couple who had been there for years. The lady said, "Mauricio, the Colón Theater looks beautiful now! It looks as good as new!" Her husband added, "I have never been to the Colón but it looks extraordinarily beautiful." I took the dessert, thanked them for their comments, and left thinking in the power of symbols as I drove across those miles I know by heart, between those two cities in the province of Buenos Aires so closely linked to my childhood.

I wondered why those two people who had a store on the side of the road had talked to me about the Colón Theater. What did it represent for them? Why, out of all the things we were doing at that time, had they chosen our work at a theater they had never visited?

When reviewing the conversation, I realized that the Colón was not a mere theater to them. It was a symbol. For many residents of Buenos Aires and many Argentines, the decadence of the Colón Theater had represented the destruction of our self-esteem as a society. Its recovery, even if they had only seen it in the media, was another symbol, and a powerful one. This was about the pride they felt over having recovered one of the best and most beautiful theaters in the world. Somehow, having concluded the work there had healed the wounded self-esteem after years of apathy.

When Daniel Chain showed me the budget estimating they'd need $300 million dollars to be invested by the city toward the restoration of the Colón, I was shocked. What was the point in investing such a large sum of money on a theater only attended by a small percentage of the population? Although this was a true symbol of Argentine culture, there was not a single contribution on the part of the national governent toward this project.

Hernán Lombardi, the city's Minister of Culture, tried to convince me, along with Chain, about the importance of doing this project, which had in theory been started by the previous administration but was then suspended amid chaos and enormous criticism. At the same time, many of the season ticket holders saw the possibility of the restoration as a threat. The project would call for the theater to be closed for several months. What if it was never finished? It was not unheard of until we arrived in the city for projects to begin and then be suspended after a while never to be resumed again.

Symbols hold a huge importance for leadership and power. With time, I increased my understanding of this phenomenon which, I must admit, was new to me. Given my profession as an engineer and my beginnings as a constructor, at first, I believed everything boiled down to investment in the project, cement, and concrete. I did not realize that I was missing something vital. It is about the construction of a story, a narrative.

Symbolic elements can build beliefs and trust in what the leader is doing. Of course, these narratives need to be supported by facts. Initially, Kirchnerism had a significant lead when it came to building a story. However, populist stories always end up promising things they can never accomplish. When faced with reality, that narrative is inevitably shattered.

The absence of these kinds of symbolic components is never good. Years after the renovation of the Colón Theater, by the time we took over the national government, we had already improved in that area. It is possible that the effort has been insufficient. Well-meaning people have pointed out on many occasions that our narrative, paradoxically, appeared to be missing a narrative. I do not believe this was true, but I understand that Argentines who believe in freedom, in the republic, and in progress, need to strengthen our narrative more than ever. At the end of the day, this is about nothing more and nothing less than being able to share our *what for*, the *what for* behind what we do, the *what for* behind our desire to be in office.

I previously have written that leadership and power result from a shared vision of future and I have learned that transforming reality calls for the incorporation of these symbolic elements. This was the reason why I finally decided to move ahead with the marvelous restoration of our Colón Theater. Hernán Lombardi's work was decisive in the incorporation of this cultural dimension. Hernán is one of those people who may appear to be somewhat chaotic, yet, at the same time, can solve many problems practically and simultaneously. At the beginning, it was hard for me to understand him. With time, his work lay the foundation of a true revolution.

When it comes to symbols, the measuring of an investment in terms of money can sometimes be insufficient in trying to understand what is at stake. It has been proven that the value of the Colón Theater lies well beyond its material aspects. It is a part of our identity, as was, on another scale, the renovation and refurbishment of the Boca stadium at the start of my administration of the club. I still remember my first walk with Mr. Seminario, the engineer at the head of the renovation work at the Colón. I felt huge anguish and my eyes filled with tears when I saw the deterioration of its infrastructure and I listened to the silence of the work suspended. It is a painful metaphor of our identity.

There is another aspect where construction work and the power of symbols meet. It is the one related to keeping one's word. We had set our minds to reopening the theater in all its splendor in 2010 as part of the city's contribution to the celebration of the Bicentennial of the May Revolution. It was a challenge that implied huge demand on the part of all those involved.

As a child, I would notice my father's satisfaction when he finished one of his construction projects. There are very few emotions comparable to saying, "It is done; mission accomplished," and handing the finished work over to the owners. At the Colón, we also fulfilled our commitment on schedule, as promised.

When the doors opened, the legendary theater had once again regained its full splendor. I felt like we were giving back to the people of Buenos Aires the pride of having one of the world's most important theaters in their own city. It was a milestone of our first term. It wasn't the only one in the area of culture. We completely renovated Parque Centenario and its marvelous amphitheater, restored Teatro 25 de Mayo, Teatro San Martín, and, above all one of my favorite places in the city, Usina del Arte, in the neighborhood of La Boca.

In the city, we fought many battles which also carried very strong symbolic and concrete components. The fight against insecurity was one of them. Since the beginning of our administration, Kirchnerists decided to weaken us at any cost. One of the most irresponsible initiatives the national government undertook was removing the federal police force from the city. Unbelievable as it may sound, that is exactly what happened.

Sometimes attacks offer us an opportunity. Thanks to the decision made at the Casa Rosada, together with Guillermo Montenegro, Minister of Security, we were able to do something completely new. It was unprecedented in the field. With Guillermo and his team, we created, developed, and implemented the Metropolitan Police. This time, it wasn't about reforming, expanding, or restoring, but building something from scratch. We drew from the experiences of many cities that had community police forces. With Eugenio Burzaco at the helm of this force, we could now count on police that adhered to the highest international standards.

Contrary to what the Kirchnerists had imagined—and contrary to the expectations of many politicians—the Metropolitan Police made a huge difference in terms of recruitment, education, training, compensation, and benefits for its members. But what is even more important is that the people of Buenos Aires realized, as the Metropolitan Police was being deployed across different neighborhoods, that the fight against insecurity could be won.

Very rarely does one have the opportunity to build an institution from its foundations. The nation tends to be a sum of patches and repairs on existing structures. The creation of the Metropolitan Police allowed us to have the police force that the people of Buenos Aires deserved. Years later, it would pave the way for the creation of the city police department, which incorporated the best practices that started with the police force we had created.

If the Metropolitan Police was a clear symbol that we are not the same as populism, the incorporation of the Green Agenda in the city was another symbolic change that modified the relationship between the residents and their city. Here too, my perspective evolved throughout my administration. In environmental matters, I initially was mostly focused on waste management, probably influenced by having seen my father's work at Manliba, thirty years earlier.

In major metropolises, like Buenos Aires, the environmental issue is extremely complex. It is no coincidence that we went through three different administrations, led by Juan Pablo Piccardo, Diego Santilli, and Edgardo Cenzón. Over time, I concluded that we needed to shift from focusing solely on waste management to embracing a new concept: Sustainability and the Green Agenda.

The need for a modern environmental policy for the city led me to approach the C40 Cities, a leadership group that we joined as part of an extensive international network of city mayors. Learning from the experiences of other cities was crucial in transforming the city into a leader in environmental and other related issues.

Many times along my journey, I have encountered a typical temptation of the Argentine political system. A desire to be original and unique in the world and invent solutions for problems that others have already faced and resolved. When I set out to make Boca a top international club, what I did was look at the world. I observed what others had done, how they had done it, what difficulties they had encountered, and how they had overcome them.

In matters such as sustainability in large cities, we had much to learn to then share and lead the transformation. It is a concept I have had since I started working. Cities and countries face similar problems. Recognizing the experiences of others and adapting them to our reality is a virtuous path toward change.

It is all too easy to narrate a successful change, such as the environmental policy, from the present perspective. However, carrying out a conceptual transformation of the magnitude we achieved in Buenos Aires was not a quick task. It was not simply about implementing government policies; it was something much broader. We undertook a true cultural change that involved incorporating the idea of recycling, making radical changes in waste collection systems, and integrating environmental education in schools. The result was tremendously positive. The Green City policy allowed us to position Buenos Aires at the forefront of the environmental efforts being undertaken by major cities.

In truth, almost none of the profound changes we made in the city were peaceful. Sometimes memory plays tricks on us along the way. I often forget the enormous resistances we had to face in the spirit of carrying out transformations. Nothing was done without challenging the constant attack of the defenders of the status quo.

Power is never exercised in a vacuum. On the contrary, it must confront those who do not want and do not benefit from change. From the very first day, there were many who were determined to boycott and sabotage our projects by resorting to all sorts of means. Still, despite the frustrations they caused me, they had one sole positive effect. They helped us grow a thicker skin. Our *what for*, our purpose, was strengthened.

19

Knowing and Knowing How to Communicate

The relationship between empathy and technical competence is one of the fundamental challenges for anyone who wishes to participate in politics. Neither condition is sufficient on its own to lead change. Neither one is enough by itself. There are no effective politicians who can sustain themselves solely based on their empathy or their communication skills. Extraordinary technicians who cannot explain or persuade their audiences when defending their management also tend not to yield good results. A good politician must possess both characteristics. Some manage to master both aspects and convey both reasons and emotions equally. They are few, but they tend to be the best.

Esteban Bullrich is one of those individuals. Esteban has acquired a monumental dimension, in large part due to the shock caused by his illness and his enormous courage in facing it. However, this Esteban Bullrich that everyone admires today is the same person I met many years ago. Back then, he was beginning his political career in Recrear, alongside Ricardo López Murphy, which led him to be elected as a deputy in 2005. In the 2007 presidential elections, Esteban supported Ricardo as a candidate for vice president. Shortly thereafter, following some differences in party leadership, he started working with us at PRO.

Since those early meetings, I knew I was in the presence of a man of integrity, ethics, and a deep sense of service. Together, we fought very tough battles that I want to highlight here. During his tenure as Minister of Education in the city and later at the national level, we carried out a true revolution in schools. Not only did we undertake numerous infrastructure projects, but we also created the Sarmiento Plan, which involved providing computers to teachers and students; we gave parents the ability to report attempts at indoctrination in classrooms; we introduced English-language teaching from the first grade; we established online enrollment; and we fought very hard to ensure rigorous and periodic assessment of educational results; something that we later implemented nationally through the Aprender tests.

Esteban always worked in a transparent and open manner, expressing his thoughts and giving his all to fulfill a central task in the administration. He not only brought about a transformation that met the expectations most families in Buenos Aires had entrusted us with, but he also established a communication style that was fully aligned with the change. His personal phone number was available to everyone. The resistance generated by the educational transformations was tremendous, especially from sectors that were beginning to lose their privileges.

That is what happened when we undertook the reform of the qualification boards that were responsible for the promotion of teachers. Until then, they had been controlled in a discretionary manner by the teacher' unions. The protests against the changes led to acts of extreme violence, including an attempt to set fire to the doors of the Legislative Palace. Despite it all, Esteban did not give up. On the contrary, as he faced each obstacle, he kept moving forward, always.

My father always built his teams by placing diversity above everything else. In a work team, everyone should be aligned around the same objectives. However, they don't have to all be the same or think the same about the same topics. Diversity requires more effort on the part of the leader, but at the same time it enriches the decision-making processes by incorporating multiple points of view. That was the reason why, in my initial cabinet in the city, I appointed Mariano Narodowski, a prestigious academic with leftist origins, as the Minister of Education.

My *what for* always tried to go beyond the old and outdated dichotomy between left and right. I am more interested in defining other axes related to the transformations that obsess me, such as old versus modern, republican and democratic behaviors versus authoritarian ones, efficiency versus inefficiency, and above all, the idea of freedom opposed to populism in any of its manifestations. I believe that Argentines have been too intoxicated with ideology, which is very often nothing more than a great factory of prejudices.

After Narodowski's departure, I appointed renowned writer Abel Posse to the position. Posse had a very strong view on the extortion by teachers' unions in their salary negotiations. He had even stated that strikes made students true hostages and the result was "as if a gun was put to their heads." He was right in many of his statements, and immediately following his appointment, the politically correct world of the city raised their guard. Initially, Posse stood firm, but after a few days, he resigned. In this case, the importance of communications skills that I mentioned earlier was evident. In order to enter the sort of Roman coliseum that is the political communication arena, one needs to have a thick skin and tolerate sometimes extreme and unfounded criticisms. Some find it easier than others. For Posse, it was impossible, so eventually, Esteban took his place.

"Do it right away!" I said in 2004 to a still very shy thirty-year old María Eugenia Vidal. I had only recently met her through her work at Sophia. María Eugenia had dazzled me with her knowledge and sensitivity to social issues. That day, she told me about her idea to implement a plan at Boca Juniors to allow 2,500 children to participate in club sports activities while also receiving educational support. That's how the Boca Social Foundation was born, a pioneering initiative carried out by the club that continues to this day.

Back then, María Eugenia saw herself as a technician in social issues and would tell anyone who would listen of her deep aversion to getting involved in partisan politics. But every time she spoke, I listened, and she managed to repeatedly convince me on how we should tackle the challenge of modern social policy in the city. She is a different person, another exceptional case who combines vast technical knowledge with exceptional communication skills. From the very first day, I sensed that she had a tremendous future in politics if she ever decided to take the leap. And finally, she did.

In 2007, María Eugenia was elected as a legislator for the city. A few months later, while I was putting together my first team of collaborators, I called her. I was sure she was the right person to take on the role of Minister of Social Development. "Thank you, Mauricio," she responded. "But there's a problem, I won't be able to take on the position." Intrigued, I asked her why, and she said, "Because I'm pregnant!" To her surprise, I told her that there was no problem and that her position would be available when her maternity leave concluded.

María Eugenia still remembers that moment. As for me, I never considered myself an expert in gender issues, but I always believed that women should be on equal footing with men in life, in business, in politics, and wherever else. Pregnancy is one of the most important and transformative experiences a woman can go through. How can it still be considered a limitation to professional development even today? I waited for her after a short period when Esteban Bullrich took charge, and in late May 2008, María Eugenia was appointed as head of the Ministry.

There, she was able to eliminate the intermediation of the picketer organizations by starting to distribute food tickets instead of the bags of food that the head picketers turned political operators gave in exchange for submission to their political structures. Years later, I saw her accomplish similar things thanks to her tremendous courage when she became the governor of the province of Buenos Aires.

No sooner had we taken office, Esteban had to dismantle the disaster that was the plan for the construction of affordable housing, which Kirchnerism and Aníbal Ibarra had entrusted to the Mothers of Plaza de Mayo and their shady representative, Sergio Schoklender, through that monstrosity called *"Sueños compartidos"* (Shared Dreams).

The insanity unleashed by our decision was such that the Mothers of Plaza de Mayo took over the Cathedral of Buenos Aires and went so far as to defecate on the altar. That was yet another example of the delusions that the Kirchnerists' war against the city government resulted in. Maria Eugenia had to cancel that scandalous scam and face enormous pressure against her. "Shared Dreams" had already been paid for 75 percent of the work without even building 20 percent of what had been promised. The national government's chief of staff was Alberto Fernández. I still remember his voice seeking to pressure me to release the pending payments. As you can imagine, time and again, I refused to endorse that insanity.

Together with María Eugenia, we created the Early Childhood Centers with the same conviction that I uphold to this day: that human development begins in pregnancy and that everything that is done in the early years will have a decisive impact on people's formation and abilities. I can still recall the criticisms we received from the supposed progressivism, which accused us of "privatizing" social policies by working with community leaders. Once again, what we did was quite the opposite.

For a long time, I had conversations with various non-governmental organizations. My goal was and continues to be for civil society organizations to become involved in politics. From the government, we were able to add the enormous management capability they have. We achieved this through many neighborhood leaders who were responsible for soup kitchens. Our policy was to expand their projects through state support by providing classroom infrastructure, equipment, teachers, social workers, and everything necessary for Early Childhood Centers to function, guaranteeing necessary management autonomy. The full-time commitment of these individuals, mostly women, all leaders within their communities, made the impact greater than what the state would have achieved in executing that task.

After accompanying me as the deputy mayor in the 2011 elections, María Eugenia chose her successor, Carolina Stanley, with whom she had worked in Social Development between 2007 and 2009 and who was responsible for the relationship with civil society organizations. Carolina continued to deepen the policies that María Eugenia had implemented in a delicate area, where we were able to leave behind decades of paternalism and clientelism.

For some time, I have maintained that social policy only makes sense in terms of its real impact. It is an investment that society as a whole undertakes with the goal of generating the greatest possible equity from the word go. It cannot become an eternal subsidy, nor should it contribute to the destruction of the culture of work. It must be assistance that helps to provide tools with a clear objective: the reintegration into the private labor market. If this is not achieved, it is not useful, and becomes little more than a band-aid solution.

Good social policy requires very rigorous studies to allocate resources that, by definition, will always be limited. That is why the priority is on early childhood. Everything happens there. When we ensure that the child arrives at school motivated and well fed, the probability of them dropping out of school is drastically reduced.

The discussions about the administration of money invested in social policies were enormous. It is impossible to solve all difficulties at once. The intention is correct, but the result is always insufficient. That is why the best investment is the one made in prevention from the beginning of life. In terms of social policy, we were able to build a virtuous dialogue in which I learned a lot from María Eugenia and Carolina, while they also learned from me. Leadership is never unidirectional. The true leader is always learning. Whoever thinks they know everything inevitably fails.

One of the tasks that I am most excited about is accompanying the development and growth of my team members. This happened with Horacio, with María Eugenia, and with countless young leaders throughout the country. When I detect potential for growth in someone, I try to do everything in my power to help them take on new challenges. That is another one of my purposes. I feel a true sense of pride when I see them consolidate their leadership. I'm sure we're going to witness what this new generation of leaders still has to offer, who with successes and mistakes like everyone else, will contribute to the definitive change of Argentina.

20

The Obstacle Machine

In the early 1980s, historian Emilio Perina published a book titled *La máquina de impedir* (The Obstacle Machine). The phrase in Perina's title is a great find and has become a part of history. It has been used repeatedly. The obstacle machine not only defines the obstacles we encounter when trying to create conditions for change but is also a clear metaphor for that tangle of obstacles that seem to work tirelessly to make us give up.

Part of my work, both in the city and in the national government, was focused on fighting against this machine. It is not a battle of ideas, nor is it about different points of view. The obstacle machine stands between doing and not doing. It has been a central component of the Argentine political culture for decades. It's the manifestation of the status quo, of no-change. It's the inertia that leads to immobility.

The obstacle machine operates through a relatively simple mechanism: any measure, any government action, any change, must be stopped immediately. The caretakers of the obstacle machine have learned something, and so have we. Change has its own dynamics. A small transformation leads to a bigger one. And this, to a greater one. For those who want nothing to change, it is essential to stop the transformation.

In some cases, it is political sectors that oppose change, just in case. In case the change goes well and then another change comes, and another, and the privileges of some end up disappearing. Sometimes, defenders of the status quo manage to stop change. For example, in the city, through the action of a small number of judges always willing to grant precautionary measures based on their political sympathies. In this way, the machine achieves its goal, which is always the same: to make everything stay the same.

The victims of the obstacle machine are not the rulers. At least, they are never the main victims. The true victims of this machinery end up being the citizens, taken as hostages and at the mercy of very lengthy processes, so that the benefit of the change never reaches them.

The list of important projects that the obstacle machine tried to stop during my administration was endless. If the opposition lost a vote in the legislature and the project was set in motion, they quickly found a way to halt it thanks to the action of some court. What is distressing is that all parties knew that sooner or later the project would be completed. Even more serious is that they knew it was an absolutely necessary project to improve the lives of the city residents.

The obstacle machine never stopped working. As I have written, for me, power is a tool for transforming reality. For them, power is a tool for avoiding change. I have reflected much on this self-destructive functioning of the political system and its effects on society. The functioning of this machine aimed to prevent citizens from seeing with their own eyes that it was possible to transform the city like never before.

People are not stupid and they became increasingly aware that change is something irreversible despite the action of the machine. That's why during my second term in the city, we were able to advance in a more determined way and overcome each of the obstacles that were put in our way. We had already discovered the secrets of how the machine works and were able to deactivate it.

An anecdote that today seems incredible happened to me in early 2008 and it stems from that old Argentine custom of dragging issues through court. It was something unheard of. I had just finished my last term as president of Boca and very little time had passed since I had taken office as mayor of the city. My focus was on my new challenge; all the farewells and the twelve years at the club were behind me. At that moment, the General Inspection of Justice Office annulled the elections in which my successor had been elected and the matter went to the courts, which determined that I should return to my position as president of Boca for ninety days, despite the fact I was the head of the city government. A total absurdity.

At the end of 2010, I had the most dramatic confrontation with the obstacle machine. This time it was not funny at all and it started in the office located opposite mine, on the other side of Plaza de Mayo, where President Cristina Fernández de Kirchner was. In early December, thousands of people occupied the ground of the Parque Indoamerican in Villa Soldati. The occupation had been organized by real mafias who had promised their victims the possibility of buying plots of land in a public park.

Those were days and nights of extreme tension, the most difficult throughout the entire time I was in charge of the city government. Upon the first complaint, a judge did the right thing and quickly ordered the federal police to clear the park. However, before completing their task, the police received orders to withdraw. Of course, the park was quickly reoccupied. It was one of the most embarrassing events in the history of the city. Kirchnerism, in its thirst for revenge against the people of Buenos Aires, had decided to abandon them to their fate.

I will never forget my desperation in those hours. I was trapped by a very strong feeling of helplessness. I did not understand, and years later I still do not understand, the irresponsible and criminal attitude on the part of the national government at that time. Soon, clashes began to occur between the neighborhood residents and the occupiers. There were stones and sticks. Firearms quickly appeared. The situation spiraled out of control and I could not do anything.

I couldn't believe that the national administration was capable of leaving the people who were defending their park helpless. As always, Kirchnerists found a false excuse not to fulfill their responsibilities. They accused us of not using the Metropolitan Police officers to clear the park. They were fully aware that at that time the Metropolitan Police lacked the size and training necessary to perform the tasks that the Federal Police Infantry Guard normally carried out.

I tried all possible contacts with the national government to get them to take charge of pacifying and clearing the park. I even asked General Secretary Óscar Parrilli to urgently put me through to the president. I never received a response.

Thousands of people had been scammed by a group of criminals who wanted to profit from a public park. With persistence, we managed to open a negotiation process with the participation of the national government, representatives of the occupiers, and the city government with the aim of ensuring the evacuation of the site.

María Eugenia played a decisive role throughout that process, which included moments of extreme tension. She managed to impose her persuasive power until the situation began to decompress. The tension we experienced in those days and nights was difficult to bear. We all knew that the danger of a widespread outbreak of violence was just minutes away.

Many years have gone by and I still cannot forgive the insensitivity shown by those who governed the country at that time. I am convinced that the occupation and eviction of the Parque Indoamericano constituted a turning point for all of us. The old politics, in their most perverse version, had presented us with the greatest challenge we had faced up to that moment. It seems like a paradox, but in that terrible context, our *what for*, our purpose, came of age.

21

On Time

As the end of my first term as mayor approached, I began to think that the time had come to attempt the next leap: to run as a candidate for the presidency of the nation in the 2011 elections. It was a bold leap. Our work in the city was still in the process of consolidation and there was much to be done.

I am an anxious person, I know. And I believed that the conditions were appropriate to take our proposal for change to the whole country. I wanted to give Argentines the possibility of choosing an alternative to the populist project that was concluding its second term. We had had four years of Néstor Kirchner and four more of Cristina Fernández de Kirchner.

In power, time management is a huge challenge for any politician with leadership aspirations. When are they ready for the next challenge? The history of our young democracy has seen many figures jump into the race before their time, only to lose their political capital and be left on the sidelines. There are always those who sweet-talk leaders, telling them that they are ready to take the next step. I always did my best to avoid them.

I had already told this to President Duhalde years before. I wanted to get there by causality, not by chance. My work has always been to build my path on solid foundations. Right or wrong, I thought that 2011 could be my opportunity to bring to our project those who saw that Kirchnerism was leading the country to disaster.

The meeting took place at Jaime Durán Barba's apartment on Alvear Avenue. It was May 2011 and the press assumed I would run for president. A few believed I had a chance and encouraged me. Others, the majority, said it was impossible to break through the tough block of voters that the president had at the time, combined with the sympathy that had emerged in some sectors of the population following the unexpected death of her husband. The electoral schedule was approaching and it was time to make a decision. Should I run? My anxiety told me yes. I had learned a lot about power and its difficulties in the early years of the city government. I believed I was ready to fight. Should I not run and go for re-election in the city? It was the safer option, but it made me hesitate. I decided to listen to all the arguments of the inner circle gathered in Jaime's living room.

The majority agreed with the Ecuadorian consultant. The chances of winning were there, but they were slim; and there was something even worse. Not going for re-election in Buenos Aires would jeopardize the continuity of our project in the only district of the country where we were in power. For those present, I was the best candidate PRO had in the city, but not necessarily a good candidate to defeat the president, whose willingness to run for a new term in office was becoming increasingly clear.

There are situations where these kinds of dilemmas arise. In these situations, taking one step forward can mean several steps back. After listening to each member of the inner circle, it was my turn to speak. "I have listened carefully to all the arguments. We cannot know today what the outcome of the elections will be if I run. We will never know. But I believe you. I would not forgive myself for risking our entire project just to take a chance. You are right. I will not be a candidate." Many breathed a sigh of relief.

The challenge was one that, in some way and on different scales, I had already faced in Boca. It was not about me. I had to set aside any narcissism. It was not just about my project. As it was then and remains now, it was about a *what for*, a purpose much larger than myself and my own leadership. I was not there to do as I pleased but to do what was best to change Argentina.

Having listened and decided not to run for the presidency in 2011 yielded its fruits. My second term in the city government was much better than the first, just as had been the case in Boca Juniors. The four years ahead of us gave us the opportunity to fully pursue our projects and neutralize the obstacle machine. The whole team had matured; together we had learned to navigate the endless complexities of administration, those which some call "the button panel," the levers that must be activated to get things done.

There are enormous differences between the time scales of the business world and those of the government. I discovered these differences the hard way; I had no alternative.

In a company, it is possible to have a high degree of control over the time variable. There, decision-making and execution speed depend on those who lead and the capacity of the people who make up its management. But in public administration, limitations are much greater. Despite everything we did in the city and in the nation, it is still necessary to make the speed of changes faster. We managed to create a public policy based on this need through the Ministry of Modernization.

The learning curves are unavoidable. This can generate a certain degree of frustration in the teams I worked with both in the city and in the nation. Moving the state is slower and more laborious than moving a company. However, with patience and perseverance, it is possible and the satisfaction is even greater. It is essential that people from the private sector come forward to contribute their experience to accelerate change in the state, as was the case with me and so many others. If we don't, the same people will continue as usual.

It is not only about time. In addition to the quantity and scale of the conflicts that are faced simultaneously, there is the cultural transformation that comes with incorporating new systems and work methodologies in teams that are much more diverse than those in a company, which tend to be more homogeneous.

Throughout my two terms heading the city government, I was accompanied by three great professionals who came from the private sector: Francisco Cabrera, responsible for Economic Development; Andrés Ibarra, in charge of Modernization; and Néstor Grindetti, Minister of

Finance. Their work was often much quieter and less visible than that of others, but they were a support and had a decisive role in the transformations we undertook. Both Ibarra and Grindetti had worked for a long time in my father's company. Pancho Cabrera had worked in a managerial capacity in large companies.

Pablo Clusellas, my legal and technical secretary, was a different situation. He is a special case since I have known him since we were both children. We were schoolmates. Pablo's role was to ensure the legality of all government actions, both in the city and in the nation. He is the person I always listened to before I decided whether to sign something or not. It is a role that requires not only personal trust but also extraordinary professional expertise. Pablo has both qualities, and then some.

In power, the relationship between friendship and work is a complex issue. Friendship ensures that trust, one of the fundamental dimensions of task delegation, is resolved. For me, the personal trust and human quality that Goar Mestre spoke to me about are essential elements to integrate a team. Both are covered by friends. But technical capacity is not a requirement in a friendship. Friendship is a bond between peers. Complex organizations such as the government or companies require vertical links. In my days as a businessman, I made mistakes on more than one occasion by appointing someone close to me on a personal level in a subordinate role, who then felt offended and aggrieved when the parity of the friendship was broken. I also made the mistake of choosing someone to occupy a position that was above their professional qualities, simply because they were a friend. These are mistakes that I took special care not to repeat throughout my political career.

The role that friends play in life is different. When they are added to a work team, the demand on them will be even greater than on others. In a way, friends are at a disadvantage and if they are in the team, it is because their professional qualities are outstanding. Otherwise, it is always better to preserve the space of friendship outside of work. A different thing is the construction of friendship based on sharing daily work. It has nothing to do with favoritism, that is, the use of friendship as a means to obtain some kind of privilege.

As my second term went by, the transformations that we were achieving in the city began to show a very clear contrast with the stagnation of the populist model that the national government was leading.

Our own political party had grown, and the succession, after my second term in the city, presented me with a new leadership challenge. It was logical and natural that different ideas, nuances, and styles would arise within a team that, despite sharing the same *what for*, would want to lead the continuity of our project. By the end of 2014, Horacio and Gabriela, two fundamental pillars from the beginning of PRO, expressed the need to resolve the internal dispute.

Internal differences are common in politics. True leadership lies in resolving them in a positive and nondestructive way. Both Horacio and Gabriela had legitimate reasons to propose their own projects. My challenge was to ensure that they did so while always maintaining the principle of unity above differences. This is the only way to ensure that internal disputes do not weaken the whole and that mutual respect is above all. I have always valued competition. Beyond my preferences, it should not be me who chose the new candidate for mayor. On the contrary, I have always thought that those who should resolve these issues are not politicians but citizens through their vote. They did so in April 2015 and Horacio was chosen to lead the continuity of our leadership in the city.

It was not written anywhere that I would reach the presidency in 2015. In fact, until shortly before the elections, my possible candidacy was ranked in an uncomfortable and distant third place in the polls, behind the two factions offered by Peronism, one led by Daniel Scioli and the other by Sergio Massa. It was necessary to build a new political tool that could avoid the dispersion of the opposition vote.

To build something new, audacity and courage are necessary. The two people who created Cambiemos with me have this in abundance. I am, of course, referring to Elisa Carrió (aka Lilita) and Ernesto Sanz. The three of us knew that in making that decision, we were profoundly changing the political map of the country.

The task of breaking down prejudices has accompanied me throughout my journey. It was present from the moment I decided to deviate from the expected path and set out to become president of Boca. Both Lilita and many Radicals had been very critical of me. They had said very harsh things. On our side, there were also voices of distrust toward the other two political spaces.

However, we quickly realized that the three of us shared the same *what for.* There are values and concepts that are at the core of Cambiemos—now called Juntos por el Cambio—which remain unchanged. I won't list them here again. My readers know them well and very likely share them too. The country where we the people from PRO, the Radicals, members of the Coalición Cívica, and so many others who joined, want to live in is exactly the same.

Without a doubt, we differ in nuances, degrees, styles, or timing. However, our *what for* is the same today as it was in those early meetings I had with Lilita and Ernesto. I have not moved an inch from those ideas and the reasons that led me to believe that the solution to our problems is beyond small discussions. A single person or a single political party is not enough, not even with the sum of all its leaders and supporters. The solution lies elsewhere.

It was society, it was the citizens who were demanding, both then and now, unity. Our role is to interpret and express the desires and frustrations of millions of Argentines. It was not just about uniting party logos and shields, setting up lists, or settling candidacies. Without a doubt, all of that would be necessary. It was about something else. It was about listening to the voices of real people, of those who get up early to work and want a prosperous future for their families, so that their children don't leave or so they can come back.

Our relationship with the other forces within Cambiemos had something of those intense courtships that quickly end up at the altar. We want the same thing, but we are different. Here too, we had to learn by doing and spent a lot of time talking, getting to know each other better, doing away with prejudices, and listening to the views of others. We knew from the very beginning that we were more than a circumstantial coalition destined to run in the elections. But in order to dream of making our *what for* a reality, the most important thing was still missing. We had to win. It's no coincidence that in those months leading up to the election, I began to spend more time visiting families with real problems following Marcos's brilliant idea of face-to-face interactions. The ability to listen is the greatest attribute of a leader and it is also one of the main necessary elements in the exercise of power. When a leader stops listening, something happens: they end up losing both leadership and power.

By early 2015, a significant portion of Argentines had had enough with Kirchnerism, its mistreatment, its abuses of power, and above all, its incompetence and the lies behind its narrative. It had been too long. The mistakes and disasters had been piling up one after another.

But above everything else, there was one main problem: the economy's variables were being sustained at the expense of the future, and very few Argentines seemed to notice this. In their daily lives, families did not perceive what was happening, yet an almost inaudible ticking could be heard in the figures of the Central Bank's reserves, in the delays in public service tariffs, and in inflation, among other central points of the economy.

There was complete and utter fiscal irresponsibility on the part of the Kirchnerist government. They were far from deactivating the macroeconomic bomb they had assembled, and as time went by, it became clear that the effects of the explosion would be devastating. The clock was set to trigger the detonator the moment the government changed, regardless of who the winner was.

The discussions among our economists during those months were very intense. A few argued that we had to move forward immediately on all fronts. The majority maintained that, should we win, we would not have enough political power to carry out all the reforms at the same time. The challenge ahead was enormous. If we won, we would have to deactivate the bomb that was about to explode and dismantle it piece by piece so that it wouldn't blow up in our faces. A part of society seemed to support the changes, but it was insufficient. Many simply wanted Cristina and her government to leave office but were afraid of the effects that the changes could have on their lives.

It is true that our agreement with the Radical Party was centered on the unconditional defense of republican values. But it is also true that we lacked the necessary time to deepen the debate about which economic model was necessary for Argentina to develop. Shortly after taking office, we had to face reality. There was no mandate from society, no votes in Congress, and no firm consensus within our coalition to face the profound reforms that our country needed.

Our weakness had a name: gradualism.

22

I Take Responsibility

On October 25, 2015, Argentines went to the polls to elect none other than the new president. The memory of that campaign moves me today as it did while it was taking place. Electoral campaigns demand for huge communicational and logistical engineering efforts, but even with all its sophistication, the polls, focus groups, consultants, and publicists, nothing can replace direct contact with citizens, that shared dream that translates into countless hugs, kisses, selfies, letters, and messages.

As had been the case with Boca and the City of Buenos Aires, the old, rusty political system once again belittled and greatly underestimated us. Marcos Peña used to reference the legend of David and Goliath, taken from the Bible and present in our culture since immemorial times, as the image of the challenge ahead of us. There, little David defeats the giant Goliath in an unequal battle. Everybody thinks that Goliath will win and they have good reasons to do so. His strength and size are incomparable to David's, who barely has a small sling. Yet David launches a stone in Goliath's face with the force of his slingshot. The giant falls and David defeats him.

A lineal interpretation could assume that I was David in this story and the deeply rooted Argentine populism represented Goliath. I do not quite agree with this idea. Argentines, sick and tired of being sick and tired, became David on that day. They fought the battle and we were merely their instrument.

That night, we went to sleep with a piece of news that left populism supporters in a state of complete shock. María Eugenia Vidal, the very same person I had met thirteen years before, had become the first female governor of the Province of Buenos Aires. She had defeated, as she herself used to call them, "the conurbation machos," that clientelism-based power that had appeared to be eternal and unbeatable. Once again, David against Goliath.

As had been the case eight years earlier, Gaby Michetti was my running mate. We came in second behind the Frente para la Victoria candidates, Daniel Scioli and Carlos Zannini, with a three-point difference, 37 to 34. It was inconclusive but they were closer to the 45 percent needed to win the election.

The days that ensued were wild. Only on two occasions had populism been defeated in presidential elections. In 1983 with Raúl Alfonsín's victory and in 1999 when Fernando de la Rúa won. In both cases, Peronism took it upon themselves to make the lives of those Radicalism presidents impossible. Both, under different circumstances, had to leave office before completing the terms for which they had been elected.

The twenty-eight days between the general election and the runoff were dramatic. Adrenaline ran at its highest level across the team. We knew we could win; we were close. The air was filled with expectation. Millions of Argentines who mobilized to vote that historical Sunday became David.

Finally, the numbers spoke: 51.34 against 48.66 percent, a small but decisive difference of 2.68 points elected me the president of the nation, meaning that 680,609 Argentines had chosen our proposal over that of our rivals. Over 12.5 million citizens had become David and had chosen the future over the past. The third non-Peronist presidency was about to begin. In 2021, I published my book *Primer tiempo (First Half)*. In it, I described in as much detail as possible my experience as president. I spoke about the tensions, the problems, and the achievements I had encountered along that marvelous and extremely difficult part of my life. That book was a healing exercise for me and, as many of the thousands of readers told me, it had had the same effect on them; on the people who had believed and hoped for change. I detailed the reasons behind what we had done and what we had been unable to do while I sincerely assessed our results in the context of the size of the challenge we had faced from the first to the last day of my time in office.

The presidential experience is something unique. It was the greatest honor I could have received from my compatriots. In some way, those four years synthesized all the concepts about leadership and power that I had developed during my experience at the company, in Boca, and in the City of Buenos Aires. I have a clear conscience because I know I did everything within my power to make our *what for,* our purpose, a reality. Still, despite everything we did during those years in government, I do not feel satisfied at all.

The time elapsed between the primaries in August 2019 has adjusted people's perspectives. The epic failure of the return of populism led the country to an unprecedented crisis. The incredible combination of fiscal deficit, extremely high inflation, international isolation, soaring public debt, depletion of Central Bank reserves and, above all, the exponential growth of poverty and insecurity, has done its job. There is no single indicator that will show any improvement in any aspect of the country. That which was good in 2019 is bad today; that which was wrong in 2019, today is even worse.

It would be a terrible mistake to settle for this. We are not good because the ones who followed us were worse. The time we have lived under the fourth Kirchnerist period, and its disasters, gives us the chance to look back on our government, to draw important learnings and lessons to apply in the *second half.*

An important part of this personal process lies in the rejection of that idea of a permanent rematch I had when I was young. The notion of a rematch, which is so important in sports, can blind a leader. We are not here to beat the other. We are here, at the company, at a club, or in politics, to lead profound transformations.

From the very first day in office, I have been responsible for everything we did, both good and bad. Life has taught me to keep an eye on the negative aspects of leadership I saw in my father. At times, he would blame his own mistakes on the people around him. This was something I always rejected. Leadership holds a magical element; it is a spell shared among human beings; it goes beyond the strictly rational. When a leader ignores their mistakes and blames them on those around them, that spell is broken. A leader must always be accountable. It is a matter of responsibility over their own leadership and others.

Unlike my father, I learned to listen. Listening is a tool that brings about security. Discovering different points of view on a matter is part of a leader's job to avoid becoming obstinate or stubborn. The leader's objective is not to be right; it is to change reality, to make projects come true, to do.

Across all disciplines, we find leaders who would appear to be more motivated by being right than by transforming things. It is a dangerous obsession that mistakes leadership with giving orders. In my opinion, listening is vital. Some saw this as a weakness in my leadership model. It is true that at times too much listening can feed the perception that decisions are diluted among different opinions, but that is not what it is about. I have never been one to let things pile up in a drawer and hope they would solve themselves. Quite the contrary; it is one of the worst traits of a leader. It only results in frustration among their teams and the degradation of leadership. If the decision-making process during the presidency turned me into a person with a greater capacity to listen, it also involved giving additional value to my own word. Leadership is not built by telling people what they want to hear. A leader is a point of reference, as is an orchestra conductor. They must always remain within the musicians' visual field. When a leader acts according to their own convenience, their leadership suffers. Political correctness, the desire to be liked, and complacency always go against the kind of leadership I value.

Agreements and consensus are important if and only if they do not betray your *what for*. Traditional politics tends to overvalue consensus, but its result will depend on the trust and value of one's word. On many occasions during my government, I sought to come to agreements with part of the opposition, with union leaders, with opposition governors. Generally speaking, they never kept their word. The pursuit of consensus at any price can be a trap when in power. Its price can mean the continuity of what was and giving up on change. We must always be alert.

Good leaders usually bring out the best in people but they cannot change the way they are or their personalities. Sometimes, there is great tension between both. It is an intrinsic part of learning. I have always tried to convey this difference to my teams. When men and women enjoy a position of privilege or power, they need to focus more intently on their limitations.

In politics, this is very clear. The wish to remain in power may lead to accepting what should not be accepted or underestimating the conflict between the transforming drive and the status quo. I have learned never to underestimate this conflict. A leadership such as the one I have tried to exercise calls for the team to be part of the solution, not the problem. I have seen many become intoxicated by power and I have also seen people who combined emotional balance with their loved ones and thus performed as true titans of change. It is about power, always. How it is used and how you prevent it from going to your head—when the latter happens, leadership becomes a horrible and destructive experience.

Trust is another key principle in my idea of leadership. A leader's task is to support, to stand behind, not at the front. They should strengthen, not boycott. Trust is vital when facing risks. The building of this bond based on trust is what has allowed me to get to where I am. It is what has driven so many people to join me and be part of this collective *what for*. Everyone must know where I will stand in every circumstance. At the end of the day, without trust, there is nothing.

I have written previously about the psychologist's perspective I have found leaders need to have but this is not enough. A leader's job is like that of a pastor, in religious terms. Exemplarity, respect, recognition, and trust are all elements present in this kind of leadership. Starting this journey calls for that magical, spiritual, emotional component that brings the whole team together and fortifies it. That bond that connects a leader to their people needs to be built on strength and solidity. When it weakens, the leader is left alone. A leader alone is useless.

The team that worked with me in my administration earned international respect, a rarity in our history. Each of its members gave their best to that project that most Argentines had entrusted us with. Any disagreement during the years in office is now in the past. As Martín Fierro says: "Know that to forget the bad is also a way of remembering." Only the first half of the change has elapsed. The match continues.

Some have been with me since the days in the city government, such as Marcos Peña, Esteban Bullrich, Guillo Dietrich, Andrés Ibarra, Jorge Lemus, Pancho Cabrera, Carolina Stanley, Hernán Lombardi, Jorge Triaca, Fernando de Andreis, Pablo Clusellas, Sergio Bergman, Alejandro Finocchiaro, Rogelio Frigerio, and Federico Sturzenegger. Others joined with significant experience in politics, such as Patricia Bullrich, Óscar Aguad, Julio Martínez, Ricardo Buryaile, Gustavo Santos, or Adolfo Rubinstein. I also brought in people who had had an outstanding performance in the private sector, such as Juan José Aranguren, Luis Caputo, Luis Miguel Etchevere, Germán Garavano, Dante Sica, Javier Iguacel, Guido Sandleris, Pablo Avelluto, Mario Quintana, and Gustavo Lopetegui. Susana Malcorra came from the United Nations and later brought Jorge Faurie to lead Foreign Affairs. I decided to give continuity to Lino Barañao as the head of the Science and Technology. Alfonso Prat Gay, Nicolás Dujovne, and Hernán Lacunza contributed their knowledge and talent to the Ministry of Economy.

They all represented only a part, maybe the most visible, of a much larger team made up of hundreds of officials who gave their all to achieve our *what for.* For those of us who were part of that journey, the lessons learned have been countless. Today, Juntos por el Cambio has an outstanding amount of experience which, combined with the strength and courage of a new generation of officials, will be the foundation to take change further and to once and for all finish crossing that river we couldn't manage to traverse in 2019.

23

Trust, Above Everything Else

I understand power as a tool toward generating change. It is, at the same time, a tool that still poses risks for the person who uses it. In my case, I have given much thought to the impact power has on people.

I have seen leaders from all fields become obsessed with their resentment, their fights, and their passions. When this kind of feelings arises, it is difficult to move on. At every stage of my career, I have faced adversaries, people who felt different about the same topic. However, I have always sought to avoid personal aggression as a way to settle differences. When a person is aggressive, they enter a destructive stage. The person who is aggressive is, above all, hurting themselves. Aggression is a problem for the person who inflicts it, never for the one on the receiving end. In my case, it worked but it took me a long time to build this viewpoint.

One afternoon in 2003 I was walking around a shopping mall. It was one of the many actions undertaken in my first campaign as a mayoral candidate. While I was talking to people who approached me and discussed our plans, I heard the enraged voice of a man insulting me. At that time, my reactions were much more temperamental and hot-blooded. I turned around and ran toward that person, who quickly began to walk away. "What's your problem?" I asked him. "Come say it to my face!" I demanded at the top of my voice. I had lost control and felt infuriated, completely beside myself. The man managed to scurry away among the crowd and when my eyes searched for him, he was gone.

I don't know what would have happened had I come face-to-face with him. Most likely, nothing good for either of us. Quite shaken, my team tried to calm me down. A while later, feeling more serene, I realized I had come very close to making a huge mistake. One should not respond to aggression with more aggression. Violence will inevitably escalate when both parties raise their voices.

Many years later, I went through a similar situation but this time my reaction was completely different. I remember I was about to cross the street during one of our routine door-to-door visits in the Buenos Aires conurbation when a very angry young woman stood before me and started to insult me. I did not immediately respond, simply listened to her for a few minutes until she paused. Then I asked her, "Is there anything I can do for you?" She was speechless, motionless. Her body language instantly shifted. Her enormous aggressiveness was still in the air and my reaction took her by surprise. After a while, she resumed her criticism but her tone had changed and the personal insults had completely disappeared.

When I worked at Sideco, I was obsessed with Benito Roggio, one of the main construction companies in the country and our rival in many requests for bids. Roggio had beaten us on various occasions, and for years, our companies maintained a strong and intense rivalry. Little by little, I realized I needed to move away from focusing on what the other person does and redirect my attention on my own job. Thus, I rid myself of that confrontation. Sometime later, something remarkable happened. When I became mayor of the City of Buenos Aires, Roggio was concerned I would use my power against him, something I had never done and would never cross my mind to do. As a matter of fact, as time went by, we built a solid friendship. This kind of personal obsessions and rivalries are always counterproductive. Letting them go is, therefore, liberating.

In politics, I learned to use some resources to clear the decision-making process of personal issues. A few days before my presidential inauguration, I summoned all the ministers to the Botanical Garden. Under the shade of the trees, we took the first photograph of that initial team, their official presentation. It was the first time I was meeting with all of them together. Many had not met each other and they were all anxious to start work. We gathered in a small room and I told them about the importance of preserving teamwork above all else.

"Now that we are gather here together, I would like to you know something. Some of you have already worked with me, but there are some who haven't. I need you all to know that the first one to bring me gossip, to talk about negative campaigning, or to badmouth a colleague will be asked to resign on the spot," I stated categorically. From the very start, I was aware that the main resource we would lack while trying to do our job would be time. To lose it in belittling the team from within is toxic, a rotten apple that spoils it all and needs to be removed completely. It would be hugely irresponsible to put personal issues above the team, especially in that context. Fortunately, everybody understood my message and I never had to honor that warning.

Another technique my team is familiar with is the one they call "the speaker method." It is one of the best and most effective ways I use to remove, from scratch, intrigues and conflicts within my teams. It is very simple. When somebody comes to me to badmouth another person in the team, my reply is always the same. I ask my assistant to immediately put me through to the person being talked about and, once they are on, I put them on speaker and say, "Hello Y, I am here talking with X who tells me you did such and such thing. Okay, now X is listening to you." Without exception, X will blush. The conclusion is always the same: they agree to meet over coffee, have a chat, and iron out their differences. Beyond the time lost in these situations, being part of a team calls for its members to be able to speak frankly with one another.

Let me say this again: Time is the scarcest asset in any transformation process. Contrary to belief, what is not done today will very unlikely be accomplished tomorrow. Some have claimed I did not administer my time in the most effective way during my presidency; they say I should have focused more on the politics, on the big issues, and not be so engaged in the day-to-day administration. I know they mean well, but I do not agree.

Many of the best hours spent in office were the ones I participated in the "sector talks." All the links in Argentina's main production chains participated in those talks, and when I say all, I mean all. Institutions and people whose actions create the cost of what we eat, what we export, what we sow, and what we produce. If the meeting was about meat, all the then governors from provinces with livestock, the producers, the ministers involved in this sector, the SENASA (National Animal Health and Agri-food Quality Service), AFIP (Federal Tax Administration), customs, the unions that represented this sector's workers would sit at the table. No one could be left out of the conversations regarding their business.

The objective behind these meetings was to jointly find ways of lowering costs. Helping the public sector and the private sector work together is a fascinating exercise. On more than one occasion, I saw how the officials were unaware of the day-to-day reality of the economic area they worked for and the same happened in the private sector: the president of the different chambers are not always familiar with the reasons and logic behind the actions carried out by the state.

These sector talks contributed toward creating a cooperative environment that sought to improve citizens' lives and contribute to the country's economy. It had never been done before; things began to change and mutual prejudices were dropped. When the question ceases to be "What can the state do for me?" and becomes "What can we do together'" my notion of power fulfills its meaning. That results in a unique transformational drive.

This honesty-based dynamics sometimes led to some uncomfortable situations. On one such occasion, we were discussing forest production, one of Argentina's many under-developed potentialities. As a matter of fact, our neighbor Uruguay, with their exemplary legal framework, has made much progress in the pulp mills sector. Logically, Argentina should hold ample advantage, but logic does not apply after so many decades at the hands of populism, and the reality is that Uruguay is way ahead of our country.

During said meeting, a union leader started to harshly criticize the existing tax system and regulations in the province of Misiones. He was very tough on Governor Hugo Passalacqua, who was present at the meeting. The union leader rightly stated that the cause behind the investment freeze in the province was the huge tax burden imposed.

After the meeting wrapped, I met with the governor who was very angry. The minute he came into my office, Passalacqua stated, "You set us up!" I tried to calm him down by replying, "No, Hugo, you are confused. The union leader who spoke is as Peronist as you are; he was simply telling the truth. Rather than getting angry, you should have listened to him. As a governor, your job is to lighten the fiscal burden so that more investments come to your province." It was pointless; despite my best efforts, Misiones did not change their fiscal demands and the much-needed investment never came.

Those forty productivity sector talks were so valuable. They were a bridge toward dialogue that had never existed in Argentina. During the second half of the change, this will have to be one of the activities more rapidly reinstated.

The first of those talks had the objective of speeding up, as much as possible, the exploitation of Vaca Muerta gas deposits. Before the 2015 presidential election, I had had the chance to talk at great length with Guillermo Pereyra, the veteran union leader for the private oil and gas workers as well as senator between 2013 and 2019. As I had done with union leaders from other industries, I proposed to Pereyra the modernization of labor agreements in his area with the objective of securing the necessary investment to transform that extraordinary deposit into foreign currency revenues. "Guillermo, if we improve your labor agreement, we will speed up the development of this sector, there will be thousands of new jobs and your union will grow." Pereyra was one of those who understood the meaning of change and the *what for*, the reason behind what we were seeking to implement in Vaca Muerta. Under the direction of Minister of Energy Juan José Aranguren, the activity grew five-fold during our four years in office.

The sector talks where we discussed the gas exploitation in Vaca Muerta was a virtuous experience. All parties involved were able to align objectives. The same happened with the mining industry, the agrobusiness, the knowledge economy, and many other areas. Each of them found an unprecedented work environment led by the president himself.

The most important value we built during those talks was trust among all members. I will never tire from repeating this: Trust is the most important driver behind the development of a society, for any initiative. Argentines have endured many decades of mutual distrust between citizens and the state, between businessmen and the government. Trust is nurtured by the value of our words and by each person's actions in relation to others. It is the element that brings us together as a society. Without trust, there is no possible future.

This need for trust is what drove me to take part in these talks. The presence of the president at all times was key. While I showed the way, I was also giving the officials the necessary support in their initiatives, as well as offering the private sector assurances regarding the value of what was being discussed. This was not a photo opportunity. They were real, joint workspaces with concrete, palpable results.

The same happened inside the administration, with countless hours spent with each of the ministerial teams in monthly follow-up meetings. My job was to listen to their problems, learn about their achievements, and help them fulfill their goals. In my view, to govern is to dedicate part of the very little time available to management and to assessing the performance of each area.

Some may have considered that this is a small task for a president, but I disagree. As had been the case in the city government, those meetings always gave me the chance to give the support I had mentioned so many times and which officials need. Contact between the leader and his team must be permanent.

My decision in favor of Marcos Peña as chief of staff, supported by two knowledgeable experts in planning and in the private sector, Mario Quintana and Gustavo Lopetegui, was based on the desire to provide all ministries with more resources, more follow-up, and more management. The same had happened in the city. Some ministers would complain over what they felt were intrusions on the part of the deputy chiefs of staff, but they had another sometimes misunderstood function. In an organization the size and complexity of the nation, it was vital to have an overall view of the progress of the change process we were implementing and, additionally, it was necessary to achieve great coordination across everybody's work. The existence of more or fewer ministries is based on order; this is not about separate compartments unrelated to each other as if they were small districts. On the contrary, the transformations we set forth required, both then and now, the participation of more than one ministry and the involvement of different teams. Team union made it possible for everyone to adapt to this work method which, following the return of populism, was unfortunately lost. The team is above individualities. When it comes to politics and public office, it is not so obvious.

Organization is key when in power. There can be no gray areas; roles must be clearly defined. As president, I was responsible for the vision, the *what for*, for steering the ship in the direction the citizens had chosen through their vote. This involves a very specific role: to communicate this vision to the team so it can become a collective and individual mission. The chief of staff is in charge of management and verifies the degree of target achievement. Each of the ministers plays a precise role: they must be protagonists and interlocutors with society and with the different actors within their specific area as well as lead the transformation of their area through a previously agreed upon plan, with terms and metrics.

The greatest difficulty in relation to time was the financial crisis following the devaluation in April 2018. Crisis have a dynamic of their own, which oftentimes become unpredictable. In an emergency, time becomes insufficient. That was, possibly, the moment when I made the biggest mistake of my administration. Power is a golden cage and that crisis forced me to devote all my time to finding, along with the economic team, a way out of the feeling of distrust that had once again taken over investors. A cloud of doubt began to expand regarding my government's chances of success, in the face of the threat of a return of Kirchnerism.

It was a very hard blow, to the point that it led me to lose my ability to listen to citizens. Many felt disappointed, lost their trust, and to a degree, they were right. My obsession was to keep the ship afloat after the impact we had suffered from the markets. It was not easy at all. My desperation between that moment and the defeat in the August 2019 primaries drove me away from part of the people. Out of all the mistakes made, this was the main one. Something was broken.

Over one year had to go by for things to improve. It took that unforgettable Saturday August 24, 2019, that brought about the spontaneous mobilization of tens of thousands of Argentines who took to the streets and met at Plaza de Mayo for me to fully understand my mistake.

Fernando de Andreis pointed to something I had not noticed. I had been kidnapped on one August 24, I took part in my first city election on another August 24, and people took to the streets to shake me up and tell me the battle was not lost and I needed to continue fighting on yet another August 24. Was it a coincidence? A message? Who knows. Regardless, it was remarkable.

During those hours, I was able to understand, as never before, the mystery of leadership. The leader and the people had distanced themselves. Yet in that coming together, the circle that had started to form sixteen years earlier, was once again closed. From that moment on, we became one again. The "Yes, we can" rallies, the passion I could feel in every city, in every town across the nation, conclusively showed me that governing is not only doing. Above all else, it is about listening.

It was during those days, hoarse-voiced, amid rallies, when Argentines taught me the greatest lesson in my political life. From then on, everything changed. Millions of citizens gave me the chance to win their trust back. Thanks to them, I was able to reunite with our *what for.*

24

The Seed of Change

Each Argentine citizen has made and continues to make their assessment about our administration. They are all valid. I have made my own. I have stood by each of my ministers in their challenges and transformations. Unfortunately, the administration that followed has not been able to solve any of the problems and, far from doing so, have worsened them to levels that were unthinkable during our government.

Our power culture proved to be different from all that we had known during the many years of populism. At all times, we made it clear that beyond victories and mistakes, our intentions had always been positive. Do, build, transform, modernize: all concepts which drove our work from day one till the day we left office.

On many occasions, I have been asked about decisions we took regarding communication during our administration. We were not perfect and I have no doubt we could have done better, both in this and in other areas. In March 2016, we published a large book that very few people have read, titled *El estado del Estado* (The State of the State). It is a detailed description, covering each ministry and each office, of the condition we found the country in when we took office. Across its pages, readers find a veritable catalogue of disasters, irregularities, and neglect. Perhaps, we did not publicize it as much as we should have, but it is also true that, unlike other governments, we did not wish to justify our actions on the legacy we had received. Still, the legacy was there: as I have stated many times, an asymptomatic disease ready to display its effects the minute we took over.

The issue of the scope and limits of the mandate as expressed through the ballots was another very significant discussion during our administration. How many reforms were Argentines ready to undertake at the end of 2015? How much change were we ready to accept? Leadership is a two-way street. It is never unidirectional. In the case of political leadership, society bears its part.

Kirchnerism did not invent populism. The populist narrative has been present among us and within our political system for many decades. Breaking away from this narrative, and its consequences, carries costs, both to those who drive it and to those who share it since it is a necessary step to leave stagnation behind. To move from the logic of a paternalist state to one that only sees to its essential duties, such as security, education, and justice, calls for profound support and clear commitment on the part of citizens.

Governments cannot distance themselves from the mandates they have received from their citizens, who are the bearers of power. I would have loved to have proceeded more quickly. Had I been able to, I would have driven the necessary reforms in the first ninety days of my administration. Having said this, would society at large have tolerated it? Naturally, I am not referring to those who voted Kirchnerism but rather our own Cambiemos voters. It was clear that those who voted for us wanted to bring the Kirchners' political cycle to an end, once and for all. However, not all the votes we received represented the willingness to conclude the long populist economic cycle.

Just how far could I, as the president, risk governance through a reform program that was not supported by most Argentines? How far could I have pushed it despite lacking the majority support? There are no easy answers here. Still, during our administration, we were able to move forward beyond expectations across many areas. This was the case with the process to insert Argentina on the world stage. I needn't detail here the number of world leaders who visited our country during our government. It had never happened before and has, sadly, not happened again since. Argentina's voice was heard and respected and, among other achievements, we led the agreement between the European Union and Mercosur which was subsequently annulled by the following administration. We were able to take our products to countless markets. We hosted one of the most important G20 summits in history. The list of accomplishments in that regard is long.

Much could be written about the changes we brought to all areas of government—transparency and open government, connectivity, telecommunications, the development of renewable sources of energy, transportation, tourism, infrastructure, not to mention the revolution we drove together with Guillo Dietrich in air transportation policy, with the arrival of low-cost airlines. At no time had as many Argentines been able to fly around the country than during our administration. They have never been able to do it again since, as a result of Kirchnerism's infinite ineptitude.

One of the best examples of going beyond the initial objectives was in the policy led by Patricia Bullrich as Minister of Security. Not many will remember this, but back in 2003 I had to face brave Patricia in the mayoral elections that took place that year. It never crossed our minds that sometime later, Patricia would be one of my best officials.

I must admit I had some reservations at the beginning. Was Patricia the best candidate for that position? We had all witnessed how hugely courageous she had been during her time as a national representative. Both Patricia and Laura Alonso were two vital players in our still small bloc in the chamber. Additionally, Patricia had already held executive responsibilities during her time at the Ministry of Employment during Fernando de la Rúa's presidency. Back then, we had witnessed her extraordinary fight against emblematic trade union leaders such as Hugo Moyano. Still, the Security position represented a huge challenge. This area ranked at the top of people's concerns, rightfully so. Drug trafficking was present in several places across the country, leaving behind a wake of corruption and the destruction of countless youngsters and their families.

It had only been a few weeks since we had taken office when Patricia announced the capture of the fugitives responsible for the General Rodríguez Triple Homicide, thus called after the town where the tortured and shot bodies of three pharmaceutical businessmen linked to ephedrine trafficking had been found. On the morning of January 9, 2016, Patricia informed me that the three fugitives had been captured by police and I made the announcement, congratulating security forces on the success of the large-scale operation that had taken place that weekend.

However, a few hours later, we learned that only one of them had been apprehended. She had got off on the wrong foot. She immediately came to the Olivos presidential residence to offer her resignation. She was sincerely regretful and it was not difficult to understand her reasons. I had specifically asked her to be very careful in handling information and personally checking that the fugitives had indeed been arrested, but her anxiety overtook her and the mistake had reflected badly on the government.

It was a moment of great tension. Still, a mistake, however serious it may be, is also a chance to learn. I rejected her resignation letter and clearly stated that I needed a change of attitude on her part when handling her anxiety. Time proved me right. Patricia went on to show she has every skill to head such a complex area.

With time, we achieved better than ever results in the fight against crime and, especially, against drug trafficking. Still, beyond the efficiency she displayed in her work, on many occasions Patricia's voice showed the right path when it came to convictions. Such was the case during the search for Santiago Maldonado, the young craftsman whose disappearance was reported in early August 2017. Maldonado seemed to have vanished following the action of the

National Gendarmerie when clearing a violent roadblock picket on route 40 in the province of Chubut. The roadblock had been set up by a pseudo-Mapuche organization.

We were suddenly the target of a despicable accusation: Kirchnerism and their associates in human rights entities maintained that the national government had implemented the practice of disappearing people that had been used during the military dictatorship. Simultaneously, political voices increasingly called to diffuse the protests by removing the gendarmerie leadership and officers who had taken part in the route 40 incident.

This was a key moment of my administration. One of the main objectives we had set ourselves was to fight drug trafficking. Thanks to the support we had granted to the security forces, a first in history, starting with the National Gendarmerie, we were beginning to see good results. Once the Maldonado affair came to an end, results were strengthened and we started to push back on the traffickers' presence across the country.

I find it hard to see innocence behind the reports and attempts to behead the gendarmerie. For me, it was a turning point. Had I chosen not to defend them, had I chosen to abandon the presumption of innocence on the part of the gendarmerie officers, my leadership and our moral authority when asking them to continue to risk their lives against the worst criminals would have been lost. I decided that until somebody produced clear evidence that supported the participation of a gendarmerie officer, not a single one would be removed from the force. Patricia stood 100 percent aligned with my decision. No member of the gendarmerie would be disciplined until we had clear proof that showed a degree of involvement with what had happened to Maldonado.

After two and a half months of searching, Santiago Maldonado's body was found in the Chubut River. The autopsy ruled that he had drowned. Those who accused us and the National Gendarmerie never apologized or retracted their slanderous accusations.

Together with Horacio, María Eugenia, and many other political figures who have grown nationwide, Patricia has become one of the most important members of our political party. I look back and ahead and I see that PRO, that dream that was born with the new century, today amasses experience, commitment, and public governance to offer Argentines a profound change as never before.

We all grew during those four years in office. We were able to resist tons of obstacles, false accusations, media campaigns, crisis, attacks, and defamation. We all gave our best. We went as far as we could toward achieving our *what for*, shared by millions of Argentines who granted us their trust.

We were not able to achieve every objective I had set. Sometimes, we were not allowed to; other times, we did not know how to, but I do feel we have sown a seed, a seed of change. During the pandemic, that seed germinated. My *what for*, that which I had discovered motionless in the small hours during my captivity, now belongs to millions of men and women across the country. Today it is present in a large part of society's identity. Unlike what happened in 2015, Argentines today want more change, not less. They want it fast, not gradual. They demand for greater freedom, not less. They call for a different exercise of power from what Kirchnerism has offered since late 2019. Argentines have also discovered their *what for.*

There is still a long road ahead, but that seed today has become a great tree and I am utterly convinced that it will soon bear fruit.

25

The Second Half

Either we are the change or we are nothing. That is much more than a phrase. It is the essence of our *what for* and it is also the conclusion I have come to after the long road I have traveled and which I have tried to share through these pages. By December 2023, the Argentine people will have chosen a new government. Following the categorical failure of populism, there is a great possibility that the new administration will be in the hands of Juntos por el Cambio.

Were this to happen, we shall have an enormous responsibility, even greater than the one we had in December 2015. Beyond the name of the man or woman who will lead the next government, there are very important aspects that will render the new experience very different from the one in the first half of the change.

The first difference lies in society. Today's Argentines are not the same as those in 2015. People no longer accept to be trampled over or belittled by power. Every time their freedom was at stake, they mobilized nationwide. In the face of absurd restrictions imposed during the pandemic, when threatened with expropriation, when they suffered extreme insecurity, the arbitrary closing of schools, the Argentine people showed they stand well above most political leadership.

The awareness of the enormous power at the hands of citizens was showcased in the many demonstrations, in participation through social media, or in formal reports in the face of attempts of political indoctrination at schools and universities, among countless other examples. This is a new society that has found many ways of making its voice heard, many of them unknown until recently.

The transformation of our society in the digital era bears an extraordinary depth. The small cell phone we carry in our hands has radically changed our behavior as citizens. It will no longer be the same to drive a radical agenda of change before a society who expresses itself independently and free of any mentoring. Listening on both parts, the government and the people, will be different. The rise of the liberal ideology has been a true breath of fresh air in the face of the monopoly of the populist narrative. Topics of huge importance in the agenda toward change, such as the drastic reduction of the fiscal deficit, state control over public order, the cost of the energy we use, or the importance of quality public education have ceased to be monopolized by only a few. Argentines are done with taboos, with what is deemed inconvenient to be uttered, with political correctness, and with fear. It has been a hard lesson to learn. Populism has brought us here through the never-ending repetition of its message, where the state is the only leading figure in our social and economic life. It is not. As a matter of fact, no one has done more to destroy and make the life of Argentines difficult through irresponsible, costly, and inefficient policies than the state.

Now, there will be neither time nor political support to do things halfway. The enemies of change will use every trick up their sleeve. We suffered from many of those tricks during my presidency. I have no doubt they will come together to try to stop the drive to transform with the objective of defending their privileges. Both the administration and those citizens committed to our *what for* must know much courage will be needed. Resistance to change will be strong, but our beliefs will need to be even stronger.

We cannot come to office with ideological prejudices of any kind. Some drastic decisions will need to be made. That "goody-two-shoes" nature that some pinpointed during our government is no more. Light populism is not an option.

The state will have other priorities. The road ahead will be outlined by the strict need to balance public accounts. If privatizing or closing down loss-making public companies such as Aerolíneas Argentinas is necessary, we will need to move forward knowing that the benefit of all Argentines is above the interests of trade union leaders and politicians. There is no point in continuing to argue that the national airline should be state-owned. Neither the country nor our sovereignty is hidden in the planes' wings, cabins, turbines, or hold. All these falsehoods have done nothing but impoverish us as a society.

Nowadays, planes are a means of transportation like any other; they're no more than buses that fly. We have proven this through the air transportation revolution we implemented during our administration. In next to no time, Argentines were able to see that low-cost companies can provide the same service as Aerolíneas Argentinas but at much lower prices and with one fundamental difference: the airfare is only paid by the passenger flying. I find it hard to imagine something more unfair than what happened following the return of Kirchnerism to power, when those who are not flying and may never get to fly on a plane must pay billions of pesos a month so that others can fly using a company managed by corrupt trade union leaders who lack any commitment to austerity or efficiency.

It may be difficult for those reading these pages to grasp the magnitude behind Aerolíneas Argentinas' squandering. The cost of this airline's six months' worth of deficit would be more than sufficient to build a new bridge joining the provinces of Chaco and Corrientes over the Paraná River, given that the existing bridge is at full capacity. This is vital to the development of the whole northeast region of our country and people living there have been calling for this, unsuccessfully, for more than twenty years.

Let's take another example in the south of the country. The city of Bariloche, one of the most beautiful destinations, among many in our country, for both local and international tourism, lacks a road that connects its airport to the city and additionally needs a new road to join the city to the Llao Llao area. The money Argentines pay to support only four months' worth of Aerolíneas Argentinas losses would be enough for both projects.

I do not wish to overwhelm the reader with figures, but it is important to know what that huge amount of money could have been used for. If we take into account the $10 billion that the company has lost since it was nationalized, a mistake of huge proportions on the part of Kirchnerism in 2008, nowadays, we could have a freight rail network to rival the best in the world, a key tool toward increasing employment across the country.

The world does not trust Argentina. I stated this in 2019 following the victory of Kirchnerism in the primaries. They turned our country into a serial swindler in the face of everyone who invested their money. Even with a 180-degree change in terms of economic policy, the world will naturally first want to see with their own eyes the sustainability and genuine commitment of the new administration. There will be no new investment in our country until we have been able to show that the change is definitive and there is no turning back.

In 2015 the world was waiting for us and welcomed us with open arms. Dozens of countries put their faith in Argentina and believed in us. Today, we only have links with the worst in the class. Nothing positive has resulted from alliances with criminal dictatorships, such as those in Cuba, Venezuela, or Nicaragua. It will be necessary to start from scratch and rebuilding national credibility will be an enormous long-term challenge.

I have already described how gradualism was the result of our weakness and not our vocation. The next government will be stronger and its strength will call for all structural reforms to take place in the early days. Poverty and unemployment cannot wait. We need to have the courage to immediately put an end to obsolete legislation in the labor, trade union, social security, and fiscal areas. That is another lesson from my presidency. What is not done from day one will very probably never happen.

The drastic reduction of public spending will need to be among the first measures undertaken. Kirchnerism's legacy will be a mammoth-sized, clumsy, and inefficient state. Each ministry, each area, each office will need to drive all the necessary reductions urgently and immediately. It will be the only way to guarantee our tax structure ceases to suffocate private enterprise, entrepreneurs, and all those citizens who make a living through honest work.

Our industries need to understand that the time to become competitive is now. The new government will not be able to continue to defend protectionism by resorting to consumers' pockets. The model of a closed-off Argentina has clearly failed. We need to build an open economy and make the most of the opportunities we have worldwide for our products, without this translating into subsidies paid by all taxpayers.

I want to state this loud and clear: the Argentine state, as we knew it, has collapsed. It is currently reduced to a giant deficit, inflation, and poverty factory. It will not just be a matter of a few cutbacks here and there; it is much more than this. There is a long list of public companies that will need to be managed by the private sector, without exemption, or will otherwise need to be shut down. Public spending has grown to such a degree that, far from being the economy engine, as postulated by populism, it has become an obstacle for the private sector, which is the only player capable of generating genuine employment and growth.

Unlike other periods in our history, we are capable of undertaking these transformations honestly and with zero tolerance for corruption. My administration's experience has shown this is possible. Technology is and will always be one of the greatest allies toward efficiency and transparency.

Juntos por el Cambio must be back in office with the objective of building true capitalism in Argentina; a land of opportunities to launch businesses within a framework of stability. With less taxes and better public services, with an independent and professional justice system, removed from politics, with well-paid and trained security forces, devoted to tirelessly fighting drug trafficking.

None of these ideas I am detailing here are new. The whole power system in Argentina is well familiarized with them. I have discussed them with governors, union leaders, journalists, and politicians with different ideologies. Many times, they have expressed their agreement. They all know the current model is obsolete and that maintaining it can only result in the situation worsening. However, our inner circle has a problem. Most of its members usually make public statements that differ from their private comments. For many of them, change means the moment of truth, the end of their privileges. This situation naturally drives them to this contradictory behavior; at the end of the day, the inner circle maintains it wants all reforms except one: that which affect their interests.

The second half will demand a great deal from society at large, but that effort will only make sense if the elites, those who have benefited from an impoverished country, are able to make an even greater effort than the rest of Argentines. The listening exercise I have mentioned, between society and its leaders, must be permanent.

Regarding social policies, one of the areas that grew the most during our government, we must do away for good with those who extort social peace. In the Argentina we will build, it will be Argentines who support other Argentines. Therefore, those who contribute their help through their work and effort will be able to monitor how each peso is spent or invested. In this second half, poverty managers will disappear. The parasitic middleman present in the distribution of help has to go. In the same way, those who receive help from the rest of the Argentines need to know that the duration of such help will be limited. They will need to train to be able to join the formal labor market as soon as possible. Both society at large and its leaders will need to take a deep look into street and roadblock pickets. Argentines have been too tolerant toward those who make commuters' lives difficult. There is no chance of continuing to witness the sad show of security forces taking no action. During our administration, we began to change this situation by preventing countless roadblocks across national routes and highways. We need to be clear: the streets belong to all citizens and they all have a right to move along them. The right to protest needs to be limited when it negatively affects others.

I have written about this before: Change is a force that exercises its pressure from the bottom up. There will be no chance of doing less than that which is expected of us. Citizens will not forgive a government that does not perform to expectation. Too many years of frustration weigh down on many generations.

In all the cities around the world where I travel either for my conferences or due to my activity at the FIFA Foundation, I find young Argentine citizens who have emigrated. I hear them and I understand them. They tell me about their lives, but inside I feel a terrible sorrow. I am the son of a youngster who left his country at nineteen to come to Argentina and become one of the leading businessmen in the country. I know what it meant to him to leave postwar Italy because there were no jobs or opportunities, and I know how he worked from the minute he arrived here. I see my father in each young boy or girl I have encountered abroad and I cannot help but feel grief for our country that lets its sons and daughters go and pushes them out because populism has robbed them of their future.

So, if you are reading this book and thinking about emigrating like so many others, I beg you to wait, to take the time to make the decision. If you stay, we will be able to fight this battle together and, if we do well, if we win, you will want to live here with your family, your friends, in your true place in the world.

I have purposefully left the topic of education for the end because it is the most important of all. Every change we undertake together starting December 10, 2023, will need to be reflected in the largest educational reform Argentina has undergone in its history. We need to reinvent our educational system. We need to put an end to the idea that the unions manage education in our country. The next government will need to stand strong against union extortion. As a result of the irresponsible closure of schools during the pandemic, a new social player has risen, probably more legitimate than all those involved in the education process. Now parents will need to sit at the table as interested parties in their children's education. They have shown they are able to, through their mobilization during the pandemic. The power equation will no longer be tied: on the one hand, the government along with parents and the overwhelming majority of teachers who wish for a better education; on the other, the strike professionals.

This is my roadmap. Through it, I have sought to express my ideas. These are but a few. Of course, there will be more. They go beyond people. The problem is not people, but ideas. Argentina's main problem is not Kirchnerism but its ideas; those that have led us to this disastrous situation.

I am trying to show a direction, a path, a plan; exactly everything that Kirchnerism has lacked since 2019. If my experience is to serve a purpose, it is to bear in mind we must be very careful about those who promise their support and then, at the time of implementing change, run away. We will always be open to dialogue and finding agreements, but if we stray away from our *what for*, our purpose, we will not have learned anything.

This is the change that I want. I know it is shared by millions of Argentines. There is no turning back and no concessions. It summarizes the lessons on leadership and power I have learned throughout many years. It is the *what for* that we need to win this second half.

Let's repeat it one more time: *Either we are the change or we are nothing.*

Acknowledgments

I began working on this book in November 2021. *What For* is the result of many hours of reflection that were useful when teaching my classes at Florida International University, Barna Management School, Georgetown University, and now at the University of Salamanca, along with other talks I have been giving around the world about my experience in leadership and power.

I am particularly grateful to Pablo Avelluto, who helped me in the tasks of organizing my ideas and sharing them in these pages. Also to Eduardo Braun and Gabriel Sánchez Zinny, who enthusiastically supported this project, providing suggestions and critiques.

Thank you to all the students across the different courses I have taught, for helping me to think and, of course, to the thousands of readers of *Primer tiempo,* who motivated me to continue communicating with them through book pages.